CARING FOR AGING PARENTS

HAROLD A. RASHKIS, M.D., Ph.D.

GEORGE F. STICKLEY COMPANY — 210 W. WASHINGTON SQUARE
PHILADELPHIA, PA 19106

CONTENTS

Part I. Fourteen Ways Of Being Old
Of these, only one seems very desirable.
Of the remainder, some are better than
others. A few seem most unattractive.
It is very confusing, but do not despair.

**Part IV. There's Also Good News:
You're Lost, But There's A Way Back**
By now you've probably figured out that
the reason why you're upset about your
parents is that you have uncertainties
about your own life.

Part V. How To Find The Answers
The answers are in the back of the book,
but they're not really useful unless
you've done the work. Anyone may
cheat if he wishes.

Preface

In an earlier book, *Understanding Your Parents*, Dr. Levon Tashjian and I talked to adolescents (and their parents) about the attitudes and behaviors of adults (particularly later 20th century American), with special concern for the way they deal with their adolescent children. We wanted to help the adolescent understand that the messages from parent to child have their origins in two separate life processes. The first of these sources is the parent's own adolescence. We also noted that many parents have lost touch with their own adolescence, much of which is forgotten, repressed, distorted, or mythified. Thus the first source is often hidden, obscure or secret. The second source is in adult reality, or in what serves as reality for the adult. The so-called "real world" of the adult emerged as a complex system of defense against the drives, dreams, and desperations of adolescence, interpersonally and institutionally developed to enable adults to go about the business of living, procreating and raising their children.

When children reach adolescence, something very remarkable happens to their parents: the feelings and impulses of their own adolescence, which had been so effectively and delicately stored, resonate to the highly

1

energetic vibrations of their own offspring, causing fragile coverings to crack away. The more dramatic confrontations between parent and adolescent child become overt evidence of the parent's inability to master not only the rebellious strivings of his offspring, but also his own, born-again adolescence.

But that is at best half of the story. Julio Cortazar said in *Hopscotch*: "The same thing happens to everybody, the statue of Janus is a useless waste, the *truth* is that after forty years of age we have our real face on the back of our heads, looking desperately backwards." But this cannot be the whole truth. There must be another set of eyes on the front of our head looking frantically into the future. For every adult knows where he or she is going: parents point the way, and will not be ignored.

There is very little time—often no time at all—between the emergence of one's children from their adolescence and the realization that one's parents are growing old. This is how life gives us the old one-two, a left to the body and a right to the jaw, with no opportunity to get set between blows.

The thesis to be developed in this book is that our use of the term "the old one-two" is not merely a low-grade literary allusion, but also reflects our observation of a natural maturational phenomenon occurring in family life. This book is directed to the mature adult who should be on "Easy Street," who should be enjoying the full strength of his and her maturity, maximizing satisfactions—and who may be doing so—but who is none-the-less caught up in the crunch between adolescent or young adult children on the one hand, and aging parents on the other. I believe there is a good reason why we get the old one-two, that the messages overlap, and that the redundancy is necessary for us to get the real message.

The real message is: "Get in touch with your own adolescence."

In *Understanding Your Parents* we explored how adolescents fail to understand their parents largely because parental communications are often not expressed in a manner their children find meaningful. There are other reasons, as we shall see. In this book I will explore the pain, anxiety, and concern—but mostly the pain—that adults experience as they become aware of and try to deal with the fact that their parents are growing old.

This is not a typical "how to" book, but when you have read it you will understand the reason for the pain, and then you will know what to do without the need for further advice.

The point is that as adults we are able to make proper decisions and to take appropriate action, provided we have the necessary information. Generally, most of us share the same information with respect to our children as we do with respect to aging parents. However, as any stamp collector knows, there is a difference between an accumulation of stamps and a collection; as any scientist knows, a difference between a casual observation and a datum; and as any psychiatrist knows, there is a difference between a delusional system and a substantiated hypothesis or a theory. Thus, there is another kind of information which is derived not from the facts alone, but from the manner in which they are organized.

And so I have revealed my strategy. What follows may to some extent be already known to you, but like some quirks in data processing, its final form may be an unexpected one. I have found it so, even though I have children and have seen parents grow old and die. It would have been helpful to have known earlier what I now know.

Some of my older friends, after reading *Understanding Your Parents*, have exclaimed, "Where were you when we needed you!" Well, here is help now.

Introduction

For the purposes of this book there are only three ages of man. There are the young, people like our children and their contemporaries, who are generally unconcerned with old age. There are the middle-aged, people like us, who have some reason to be concerned with old age, and then there are old people. Old people may be defined in three ways. First there are those who have been living a long time, say eighty years or so. Then there are those who, regardless of age, feel old. Finally there are those who, because of their behavior, are considered by others to be old.

Old people are all around us, yet unless they become a matter of special interest, we may not notice them or the conditions of their daily lives. Most of us have, or have had, an elderly relative. We have observed, perhaps thoughtlessly, old people in the community in which we live. We have read books, heard stories, gone to plays or movies and have thereby acquired some sense of the options facing the aged. In Part I of this book I consider fourteen situations in which old people may find themselves. In order to accentuate contrasts, they are presented in pairs. This presentation is intended to establish a common ground on which we can appreciate the situations and

5

their implications for other family members—when there are family members.

Part II confronts us with the realization that one or both of our parents is growing old and that certain decisions will have to be made. This awareness will make the situations described in Part I relevant. They move into the foreground of our consciousness; they bring us a message.

The realization that our parents are growing old comes as a shock. It is a shock whether we have been actively engaged with them, or if we have been ignoring them, taking them for granted, perhaps seeing them only on ceremonial occasions such as holidays, weddings or birthdays. If actively engaged, we are shocked that they shall have to withdraw, leaving us poorer and weaker by their parting. If we have been moderately estranged from our parents, we will be shocked by a flood of new concerns, anxieties, resentments and memories that are oddly out of focus. In either case we will have to think about things that we did not want to think about, have feelings that we did not want to feel, and make decisions we have forgotten we would have to face.

Things get worse before they get better. In Part III it is proposed that we don't like to think that our parents are growing old, because of the implication that we too will grow old. While our parents are alive and well they serve as a buffer between us and death. When they grow old we know that they will die—and we are next. While in an objective sense we know that this is true, it is not the sort of thing one cares to contemplate as an imminent event.

Part IV reaffirms that our dismay at our parents' decline reflects our own insecurities, our own dissatisfaction with where we are in life. But it also proposes that we are not immobilized, and that by anticipating our own old age and eventual death we will be able to cope with the death of our parents. If we need help, it assures us that help is available.

Finally, Part V unravels the knot, showing that there are answers, but that the answers make little sense unless one comprehends the issues raised earlier in this book.

None of the answers is likely to be entirely satisfactory, however. Decline, decay and death are not sources of joy. Our solutions do not resolve, our decisions are not painless. In Part VI it is suggested that there are circumstances in which our old parents can be helped further, and, parenthetically, that there may be help for us when it is our turn.

The Epilogue reviews the journey we have taken. After debriefing we will have to embark on the next one.

PART I

Fourteen Ways of Being Old

Of these, only one seems very desirable. Of the remainder, some are better than others. A few seem most unattractive. It is very confusing, but do not despair.

1

If There's Room In Your Heart There May Not Be Room In Your Home.

The first pair. *Sally G.'s mother has her own apartment; Norma B.'s mother is in an old folks home.*

Sally G.'s mother is 92 and lives in her own apartment. She is bedridden, incontinent of both urine and feces, and is mostly incoherent. What she does have to say is usually hurtful. There is a cleaning lady who comes in for a few hours every day, and there are practical nurses around the clock. Sally, an only child, visits her mother nearly as often as the cleaning lady, and with greater regularity.

Those who know Sally well have heard her complain about having to see her mother because of the abuse she gets with every visit. She resents going, and wishes that her mother would die. "She's a nasty old woman," says Sally, "and is of no use to anyone, including herself."

There are several ways of looking at this situation. First of all, it is evident that the expense of maintaining Sally's mother is considerable, requiring an income in the upper two percent of incomes for all U.S. families. It is also clear that no love is expressed between Sally and her mother.

But another way to see this situation is as the best of all possible solutions for Sally and her mother. With respect to physical care, this is a valid judgment. But it may be more difficult to visualize the absence of love as a desirable aspect of the relationship. But Sally and her mother do not view love in the usual way. For them, love is a commodity, a giving which requires something in return. Sally and her mother are wealthy, and their wealth was not acquired by giving something away for nothing. Hence, if love is a commodity it must be bought and paid for. If one receives love and gives nothing in return, one is in debt. In the economics of affection, this undesirable condition yields a product known as *guilt*, a very unpleasant subjective state. Guilt does not eliminate the love-imbalance, and is entirely useless.

It must be recognized that Sally's mother is going to die, and it is very important to her and to Sally that she die with the emotional books in perfect balance. There may be no outstanding debts; neither may owe the other. This also means that there will be no guilt. It is very desirable for Sally's mother to die without guilt and for Sally to feel no guilt after her mother is dead.

So Sally and her mother have a comfortable arrangement: No one gives, no one pays, no one owes, no one feels guilty. Sally's mother need not feel bad about staying alive or dying; when she dies, Sally will not have to mourn her.

This is the way that Sally and her mother have worked things out. Some of us may not be comfortable with such an accommodation, but each of us will have to work it out *some* way. Have we managed better? *Will* we manage better?

Norma B.'s mother is in a home for the aged which is supported principally by religious charities and governmental funds. She receives good care overall. Norma has a husband, three children, and a full time job, and she manages to visit her mother every day. She never complains. Her mother would like to be living with Norma, but to the best of her ability accepts that her daughter's circumstances make it impractical. Thus, she generally manages to avoid criticism of the home, and catches herself when on the verge of saying how nice it would be if she were with her family.

Both Norma and her mother spend a lot of time feeling guilty. Norma feels guilty that she's unable to keep her mother at her home. Her mother feels guilty because Norma visits every day in addition to having a job, home and family, and also because she really doesn't like the home and wishes she could leave. Norma's mother grew up believing that one should be content with one's lot; Norma grew up with the same conviction.

When Norma and her mother talk, they always find nice things to say to one another, both avoiding the painful issues of reality.

When Norma's mother dies, Norma will take it very hard. She will not only feel sad and guilty, but will go into a serious depression requiring psychiatric treatment. Her husband and children will pass through a very difficult period, from which they will learn nothing useful.

*   *   *

The conclusion to be drawn from these cases has to do with love and death. They do not go together. Love is for the living. Dying becomes easier as love is withdrawn.

The case of Sally G. and that of Norma B. were chosen because of their contrast in affectional quality. Norma B. and her mother are warm and loving. Sally G. and her mother are cold, formal, and distant.

But Norma and her mother are emotionally bound to each other. They cling together in their need for emotional support. Separation is extremely difficult for them.

Sally and her mother long ago achieved separation. Each could face the world without the other. They are both adults. If they liked each other it would be pleasant, but it is not required. Thus Sally G. is in a much better position to face her mother's death than is Norma B.

2

Maybe Having Them In Your Own Home Makes The Difference.

The second pair. *George F. is part of the family; Sophie T. makes trouble.*

George F. is a widower, eighty-one years old, and lives with his son, George F., III, and his wife Polly. Polly is crazy about old George, pats him or kisses him whenever she passes near, and calls him by his nickname, "Whacker." Polly and her husband can't recall where old George got his nickname, but it certainly wasn't for beating the children. It might have been from cricket, which George hasn't been able to play for quite a few years. Old George for decades had been master of the hunt, and this virtually hereditary title had passed on to George III. Even today George and Polly wouldn't dream of buying a horse without consulting "Whacker."

After the fire at Chadds Farm which took the life of young George's mother, old George wanted to rebuild, even though he was seventy-eight. George and Polly had a smaller place, and insisted that old George live with them. This was quite practical with no loss of comfort, but old

George, feigning reluctance, demurred. But their persistence and his desire to be near his grandchildren persuaded George. It worked out marvelously well.

Old George was very envious of his son, for he had always found Polly very attractive. Although he had adored his wife, he also had a yen for Polly's mother, though no one knew for sure if anything had come of it. In any event, he loved Polly, but not as if she were his own daughter. George F., III, was as nearly oblivious of all this as one could be, short of acting the total ninny, and was quite content with his work and his family. In turn, Polly was so charming that no one could have the slightest notion of how she felt about anything.

*   *   *

Sophie T. also lives with her family, but it wasn't their first choice. Sophie would have preferred to remain in her own small home, which was paid for, but the expense of upkeep and her own diminishing capabilities were deciding factors. Sophie had three sons. The youngest, Bob, was the only one who seemed much concerned with her welfare. The oldest had problems of his own; the middle son was definitely hostile. Sophie wailed. "Three sons, and no one gives a damn about his old mother!" Well, Bob gave a damn, and complaining all the way, invited his mother to come and live with him, his wife, Clara, and their two children. Bob and Clara agreed it would be cheaper to have mother move in with them, especially since Sophie was on the verge of needing help in her own home.

Sophie's mother had had a low opinion of men, and Sophie grew up in the environment generated by that attitude. Accordingly, her expectations of how men would treat her were mostly negative. Her father and husband didn't actually treat her badly but, *expecting* bad treatment, her perception matched her expectations. Sophie's sons thus grew up confused about their own goodness, since Sophie was endlessly critical of them. Sophie was herself confused about the maternal love she felt, and for the most part managed to keep from revealing it to her boys.

Bob grew up not talking very much, and was known as still-water-that-ran-deep. His explosiveness concerning the decision to take Sophie into his home was that of a man foreseeing his own doom.

Clara was by no means a silent woman, and made it clear to Bob that it was *his duty* to take Sophie into their family.

The outcome was disastrous. Sophie became a part of the family. The family became a part of Sophie. She sided with Bob, she sided with Clara. She sided with Bob and Clara against the children, she sided with the children against Bob and Clara. She sided with the boys against the girls, and with the girls against the boys, settling ultimately in the latter position. At one point, Bob threatened to move out, but Clara, whose instincts about men were more useful than Sophie's, managed to keep the family together. The story is not over yet; the struggle continues.

*   *   *

There are striking differences between these two situations. Obviously not everyone is as charming as George, his son and Polly, nor as fractious as Sophie, Bob and Clara. And since people and situations differ, it is evident that keeping aging parents in your home is not always practical. Sometimes it works, if there's enough room and you're all compatible. But if powerful destructive forces are operating, even if—indeed, *especially* if—they're unconscious, the best plan is to preserve distance. This means that parents have to be kept either in *their* home or in *a* home.

3

Some People May Be More Lovable Than Others.

The third pair. *Everybody loves old Henry P. but Sara W. is equally beloved.*

Most people who have heard of Henry P., including those who have benefited from his philanthropies, are not sure how he made his money, but he made a lot of it. And no matter how hard, unscrupulous or dishonest he might have been in his business dealings, he is today perceived as a warmly generous person.

Henry appears to have no family, but he can hardly be said to live alone. His home is a castle completely staffed with servants. There are always at least six of Henry's retainers on the premises, and there are constantly two on duty, for Henry never sleeps more than an hour or two at a time, and he requires someone talking with him or reading to him throughout his waking hours. He cannot read or watch television himself since he is nearly blind as well as bedridden. He enjoys good literature and his store of knowledge is impressive. Occasionally, but with diminishing frequency, he delights in being a Dirty Old Man, but those who have served his needs and desires find this unobjectionable because of the directness of his manner and his warm gratitude. "It continues to be part of my life," says Henry.

Henry also has a constant stream of visitors. While many of these seek financial support for one project or another, some ask only for words of wisdom. No one leaves empty-handed. Not everyone who requests money gets it, but all get good advice. No one leaves completely disappointed.

Put simply, Henry needs to have his conscious mind engaged at all times. When his mind is fatigued he falls asleep. Sometimes he falls asleep when he is bored, but more often he requests a change of topic.

It is never appropriate to ask Henry how he feels. If something hurts him he will tell someone. If he enjoys something he is not diffident about making it known. However, one would not ask Henry if he is happy, or even content. His answer would be that he was not being asked a substantive question, that it did not concern a matter of fact. Of course, if he were asked for an opinion, he would say his opinion would be biased and subjective and, he would add with a wry smile, there could be no counter-balancing opinion, for no one else would be in a position to offer one.

*　　　　*　　　　*

Sara W. also lives in a big house, but it does not belong to her, and she too is never alone. Indeed, more people live in the house than the law permits, but despite legal injunctions, they continue to remain because they have no other place to go. Sara, like Henry P., is bedridden, but she is not blind. However, since she never learned to read, Sara loves to have people read to her as often as possible. Her interests are no less catholic than Henry's. Without money, Sara pays her readers and all others who care for her with good talk.

Sara is a natural resource, a great reservoir of common sense. She would be a worthy subject in any scientific investigation of heredity versus environment. For Sara is not just "street smart"; she has a profound grasp of inter-personal relationships. She knows the messy little games people play with one another, and her mind cuts through them like a hot knife through butter. She has no grasp of science, international relations, or economics, apart from those aspects that can be reduced to the interpersonal.

Since people generally are more interested in gossip than in history, Sara's intellectual deficiencies go un-noticed. Soon Sara will be ninety-five. There will be a camera crew at the home from one of the local TV stations, and a reporter will interview Sara on what it's like to be ninety-five, with no living relatives. And Sara will say, "Honey, so far as I know I was born an orphan. God put me here, and if He's willing I'll see a hundred. Come check on me in five years." This retort will rattle the TV reporter, who has no idea what *she* will be doing in five years.

*   *   *

Thus we have two individuals of obscure origin, one rich, one poor, both verbal and clear in the head. It might be argued that visitors go to Henry P. because he has money and they hope to get some of it. But visitors come to Sara W. because she makes sense and is without pretense.

There seem to be several bottom lines. The first and simplest has to do with how much money you acquire. The second bottom line is whether people are attracted to you, because of your money or for other reasons. But there is a final bottom line: *Who* comes to you? Are your visitors people who are significant to you, those with whom you can share feelings, and with whom you have common associations? Henry P. comes out well on the first and second bottom lines, Sara W. only on the second. Does either score on the third? I think not.

4

Money Must Make The Difference.

The fourth pair. *They'd like to kill Paul O. They did kill Samuel B.*

When their children appear to have been raised successfully, it is a pleasure for parents to take credit for having supplied good genes, a good home and a good example. But when sons and daughters reach biological maturity unable to maintain an organized life, capable only of spending money, doing poorly in competitive activities, while using sex, drugs and liquor destructively, a parent may find it convenient to look the other way and to blame external influences for his children's misdirected development.

Paul O. tried to do things right, but he chose the wrong woman to bear his children: she was alcoholic and compulsively unfaithful and he divorced her. She was not considered fit to raise the children, so they passed through adolescence without a mother, except for a brief time when Paul was married to a much younger woman who then left him.

Thirty years later, Paul is in his late sixties, retired, di-

21

vorced for a third time. His daughter, Lucy, 45, has been divorced twice. His son, Walter, 42, has never married, and works without ambition for an investment firm. Lucy and Walter are chronically in debt. Paul gives both some money, but much less than they feel they need. Because of their inability to achieve separate lives, all three live in the same house. There is little interaction, especially between Paul and the children.

Lately Lucy has been talking more with Walter. She complains about her lot, he complains about his. She blames it on the way they were brought up, and Walter enthusiastically takes up the chorus. Lucy tells Walter of his dissatisfaction with their father, to whom she refers disparagingly as "King Lear." Together they think of the estate he will leave, and wish it would come to them soon. Lucy and Walter agree that it would be nice if they could speed his death, and fantasize about killing him. Neither has the guts to commit murder, and the conspiracy leads to a falling out. He calls her "Lady Macbeth"; she calls him "Hamlet." They stop talking to each other and go their separate ways.

*   *   *

Samuel B. used to work for the railroad and now survives with his daughter and her four teenage children. When he dies he will leave several thousand dollars in death benefits. Since Samuel is a widower, the death benefits will go to his daughter, who currently survives on welfare. The children are also included in the welfare payments, which they supplement by stealing. They steal because income from work would reduce the welfare payments, but more importantly because they prefer stealing.

The teenagers' mother, Betty, has been drinking and using drugs more heavily. She has been cooking less, and Samuel who is unable to fend for himself, has been getting very little food. Eventually he will starve to death, but Betty is impatient. She resents the little food he eats.

The loving kindness and respect for the rights of others that Betty may once have had have now been obliterated by alcohol and drugs.

One night Betty offers Samuel a drink of whiskey and gives one to her oldest son. Then, in rapid succession she gives Samuel two more drinks and she and her son drag him to the top of the stairs. Betty pushes him down. When he reaches the bottom, Samuel's grandson hits him on the head with a bottle. "Make sure he's dead," says Betty.

*   *   *

These cases are extreme in that they represent behavior which is foreign to most of us. But do we not often *wish* others dead, including members of our own family? It is not uncommon to want one's parents to die, and not always for humanitarian reasons.

To be the object of murderous thoughts, occasionally of murder itself, is a condition of old people's lives, thus it cannot be omitted here.

More broadly, the aged are a class of people for whose death society is waiting expectantly. To the extent that the aged are seen as a "problem," some individuals will tend toward a "final solution." The issue is an ugly one, but it is also unavoidable.

Could It Be Love?

The fifth pair. *They do everything they can for Ruth D., but things go better for Cora Y.*

Ruth D. is only sixty-eight years old, but since the death of her husband three years ago, she has become increasingly senile. Astute observers among her friends and family point out that even before his death she was often confused and forgetful, covering her awkwardness with a little laugh, while her husband would supply the missing word or phrase, or take her arm to make sure she turned in the right direction. Now there is no one to maintain appearances, and her deterioration is evident.

Ruth's daughter, Peggy, is the "responsible relative," and wants to do everything possible for her mother. There is no doubt in Peggy's mind that Ruth must be maintained in her own home at any cost. Peggy's siblings do not share her conviction, believing that Ruth would be better off in a nursing home, and refuse to make financial contributions to the enterprise. Peggy's husband worries about how they will make ends meet with two children in college. He is feeling the crunch. But because of his love for Peggy, he is willing to accept that what Peggy wants for her mother is best.

There is a naive, dependent quality to Peggy's husband that attracted Peggy and that her mother thought would make him a good husband. But his kindness is leading the family into bankruptcy. He wants to do the right thing, and assumes that Peggy understands their financial situation. But Peggy doesn't understand finances. She too is naive, believing that doing what seems best will make everything come out right.

It isn't long before the children in college have borrowed all the money they can, and Peggy's husband has to take out a bank loan to help them further. Neither Peggy nor her husband has had any new clothes for a year, and they pray that nothing will go wrong with the house or the car, but their prayers don't seem to help. The only steady state in the family is that of Peggy's mother, whose deterioration appears to have levelled off. Her general health is satisfactory, and it looks as though she might live for many years.

Peggy and her husband are pleased that Peggy's mother is doing so well in her own home. Unfortunately, they don't seem to realize that while they're supporting Peggy's mother's home, they are about to lose their own.

*   *   *

Cora Y. had six children, three sons and three daughters, all of whom grew up and established their own families. She was eventually left as a widow, alone, with very little money. Cora continued to work, as she had all her life, well into her seventies, neither telling anyone her age nor reporting her income. Increasing arthritis, especially of her hands, ultimately put an end to her productive years.

Cora had always valued her independence, but at Thanksgiving dinner, to which she had invited her six children and their families, she announced that she would finally have to give up working and, soon, give up her house as well. This announcement was greeted by an enthusiastic chorus of cheers along with invitations of, "come and live with us." The outpouring of affection and acceptance was quickly resolved by Cora's agreeing to spend several months a year with each of the families. Action followed plan, and many grandchildren were made happy and their lives enriched by Cora's stories, wisdom, and good cooking, all reflecting the love she freely gave and received.

*   *   *

It is obvious that Cora and her children are healthy, and equally clear that Peggy and her husband are making two big mistakes. Peggy's mistake is in thinking that her mother should stay in her own home, while her husband errs in thinking that his wife knows what she's doing. Of course some will agree that Peggy is right and that she has a good husband. A great deal hinges on how long Ruth D. lives but actuarial thinking is appropriate for insurance companies; Peggy and her husband are unwittingly gambling on Ruth D.'s life expectancy. They are in no position to gamble, especially blindly.

There are underlying reasons why Peggy feels as she does, just as there are underlying reasons for her husband's attitude. Explanation is like dealing with a tangled string. You untangle as much string as you need at any time. Later on we can untangle some more.

6

Could It Be Guilt?

The sixth pair. *Sonia Z. lives much better than Mary A. but it doesn't feel any better.*

Sonia Z.'s situation superficially resembles that of Ruth D. She lives in her own house, is becoming quite senile, and her children contribute to her support. But she has several children who contribute, and none is stretched financially as are Peggy and her husband. Nevertheless, the contributors to Sonia's welfare are making sacrifices, and only one of them can claim her as a tax deduction. The benefit resulting from this privilege is shared among them in the form of a lottery, the one small satisfaction to be derived from an otherwise awkward situation. For Sonia, despite her failing intellectual powers, not only manages to ask for her children's support, but *demands* it, as she made demands on their late father, doubtless contributing to his early death, and as she made demands on them as they were growing up, and as she made demands on her brothers and sisters, who no longer respond to her emotional summonings.

29

As a result of Sonia's demands, her children see her only occasionally. The oldest son takes responsibility for managing the finances. He has power of attorney, and no longer needs her signature for documents.

A consequence of the emotional distancing is that Sonia has contact only with the help in the house, to whom she refers as her "keepers." She believes that they steal from her and take poor care of her and the house. She is probably correct on all counts, and struggles to convey this to her oldest son. He manages not to understand, choosing to find her words unintelligible and her speech rambling—which it often is, though not devoid of meaning. Thus Sonia is enormously frustrated. She is no longer able to control anyone, and can't adequately file her complaints. Although her home is comfortable and her material wants and needs are satisfied, Sonia wishes that she were dead. But no one is aware of her true feeling, and she goes on living, to the apparent benefit only of her "keepers!"

*   *   *

In contrast to Ruth D. and Sonia Z., Mary A.'s children decided that *in no way* would they try to keep Mary A. in her own house, and *in no way* would she live with any of them. Thus Mary now resides at Wysteria Manor, where the high point of the day is just before dinner, when the ambulatory "guests" gather for a drink of sherry, or something stronger, in the Blue Room. This custom is resplendently advertised in the Manor's brochure, and some who read it wonder if it wouldn't be just as well if the "guests" stayed snockered all day (there are those in management and among the "guests" who strongly agree). Mary is not a heavy imbiber, but she is grateful for the custom, since the cocktail hour is the time for an infrequent family visit.

Except for the Blue Room, there is not a great deal to recommend Wysteria Manor. The rooms and food are of the quality of a mediocre motel, and the standards of professional services are not high. Canned music leaks through the halls, accompanied by shouting or mumbling from TV sets left on throughout the day and evening. Occasionally a scream or a shout is "live," eventually attracting the attention of a staff member. Probably none of the staff is intentionally cruel, but occasionally they are hit or bitten and respond reflexively. Many rooms stink of urine or feces.

Mary feels that her family has disposed of her. Her family also feels that they have gotten rid of her, but occasionally a family member is burdened by guilt. This is when he or she visits Wysteria Manor to join Mary for a drink in the Blue Room.

*   *   *

The circumstances of Sonia Z.'s life and that of Mary A. represent reasonable solutions of what to do with Mom or Dad after they have been widowed and have become old and feeble. Either solution is acceptable and, if anyone is watching and grading our efforts here on earth, we will probably be given partial credit on the What To Do With Your Old Parents Test of Intelligence and Social Judgment. The problem with these solutions is that, while "correct," neither works very well.

It might be argued that the real problem is that both groups of children are putting their parents out of the way. Yet I hasten to point out that both of these ways are condoned—indeed lauded—by our society. Or, it might be suggested, the *deeper* problem is that the "kids" (middle-aged kids!) are selfish, visiting their parents only out of guilt. But it should be noted that selfishness is encouraged—even praised—by our consciousness-raisers, and if there weren't a little guilt, parents might not be visited at all.

If there were less guilt and more concern, parents might be visited more frequently, but quite probably not a great deal more.

Thus we must conclude that these "solutions" do not solve the problem, but ease a situation that might otherwise be even more unpleasant for all concerned.

7

Then It Must Be Sex.

The seventh pair. *Ben G. makes his own way. Olga R. is glad he does, but not always.*

Ben G. is a sexy old guy. He has outlived several wives and most recently had a live-in roommate young enough to be his daughter, or even grand-daughter. She left simply because it was time for her to move on. Ben doesn't think for a minute that she left because he's not sexy enough, for their couplings often left both of them exhausted.

Ben still runs his business; he's a manufacturer's representative ("Rep," he says, "as in reprobate," with a chuckle). He has his own place, frequently sees his kids and their kids, travels, swims, plays golf and tennis, and tells everyone that he expects to die in the arms of a beautiful woman. (Some beautiful women have had the same thought and have accordingly turned him down.)

Olga R. was a friend of Ben's last wife. A widow, she lives with her daughter and son-in-law. A little younger than Ben, she lacks his physical vigor, but longs for companionship. Lately Ben has been looking for a woman nearer his own age because he thinks he might be more comfortable with her. A chance meeting between Ben and Olga's son-in-law resulted in a dinner invitation, and the connection was reestablished.

When Ben and Olga went out on their first date, Olga was absolutely terrified, and Ben decided to move in on her very slowly. Nevertheless it wasn't long before he invited her to his apartment for dinner, and not much longer before he had her staying all night.

Olga's fears having been overcome, she revelled for a time in her newly rediscovered sexuality. Her energy level was far below Ben's, but she did the best she could. It was not long before she began to feel possessive of Ben, and insecure as she was in the realization that his desires were stronger than hers, jealousy reentered her life. She was certain that he was seeing other women, as indeed he was discretely, changing the subject when Olga raised questions.

Finally Olga managed to corner Ben, who responded that she was acting like a nagging wife and that he would see other women as he pleased. Olga took this badly telling Ben that, if he saw other women, he couldn't see her.

Things rested there for a time. Olga's daughter and son-in-law knew that there was a problem, but decided to keep out of it. Ben felt bad that Olga felt bad and managed to get her to talk to him again. He presented his philosophy of life, which was simply that each of us should get all the pleasure we can, and not begrudge others their particular pleasures. Olga gave this some thought and concluded that it sounded reasonable, although something about it bothered her. Since she couldn't focus on precisely what was wrong, she decided that it must be all right.

Unable to muster arguments to the contrary, Olga agreed to spend another night with Ben, agreeing to have sexual relations, even though she remained troubled. Her effort to relax and let everything go caused her to lose bowel and bladder control and in great embarrassment she went home.

Since this episode, Olga's deterioration has been evident to her family and friends. Ben was also shaken by the experience. He has wanted to see Olga, but she will not speak with him. He too is depressed and fears he will soon start feeling old.

*   *   *

I am open to criticism for including Ben G. among these seven pairs of vignettes. There is no doubt that he is a "ringer" in the sense that he is merely chronologically old and is in no sense a dependent. His family does not have to worry about him, at least not yet, and he makes his own choices about the circumstances of his life.

There are many old people like Ben, living alone or as couples, but this book is not about them, since they are not problems for their middle-aged children.

Indeed it is important to separate, at least conceptually, older people like Ben from older people like Olga. Ben is still very much in this world; Olga's grasp on it is more tenuous. Indeed it might have been better to have kept Ben away from Olga altogether, but how do we do that? Can middle-aged children stop an aging parent from dating? Wouldn't that be overprotective? What is the etiquette of old age?

8

What Is The Answer?

Life impresses with its diversity, but there are ways of looking at it that can be useful for each of us.

The preceding chapters have described various situations in which old people live. No attempt was made to be inclusive, and only "single parents" were considered. Perhaps this restriction represents a prejudice on my part: if both parents are alive and living together, though they may need help at times, the pressure on their middle-aged children is much less than when the latter become fully responsible for a single aged parent who is more or less incompetent. It may seem that the rich are over-represented, but as I will explain in Chapter 24, they are, according to my scheme, actually under-represented. The poor are also under-represented, but for the same reason as are the rich, so there is no discrimination.

Except for old Ben G., none has an easy time of it. Each one has a definite limitation: life has wounded them all in some way, physically, emotionally or both, and this is why they pose problems to themselves and to others.

The Angel of Old Age passes over all our houses, and no one is spared, apart from those who die young—an ordinarily unattractive alternative, though chosen by some.

Reading through these vignettes, and thinking of your own parents, certain situations may seem more plausible to you. Others will seem remote from your experience. But there is no need for a decision here; my purpose is to suggest that *there is not a right way for everyone*, or perhaps no right way for most. Nevertheless, some solutions may be better than others, at least for a time, and in the following chapters we can explore some of the factors involved as we determine what to suggest to our aging parents. Of course they may have other ideas, and we will all have to deal with that. I'll try to be of some help.

PART II

Your Own Parents Are Getting Old

Bringing it all back home, you can see
that your own parents' lives will have to
shape up in one of fourteen ways. But
which one?

9

You're Becoming Uneasy.

Even though everything may be going fine in your own life, something is troubling you. You know what it is.

It is nearly time for you to make a decision about your mother or your father. After recovering from the grief of having been widowed, she or he continued to live in the same familiar home and managed well, keeping up interests in hobbies and in social and community activities, perhaps spending significantly more time visiting with you, but essentially making it alone. You didn't spend much time thinking about their future, except when something happened to remind you that old people often cannot continue on to the end of their lives living by themselves. Perhaps the couple with whom you play mixed doubles every Saturday afternoon recently had to put one of their parents into a nursing home, or possibly the bookkeeper at your office had to take a larger apartment so that her mother could move in with her. Or maybe you watched a television special on retirement communities, or read a report from the Hudson Institute predicting that the year

41

before the Earth runs out of fossil fuels, 99 percent of the population will be 65 or over. Indeed, every time you hear the word "old," instead of thinking "Granddad" or "Very Special Pale" you find that you think "Mother" or "Father."

What will you do? While they may yet be in reasonably good health, their memories are failing and they do not always think to look both ways before crossing the street. You wonder if they remember to eat their meals on time, or take their medicine, or even to change their clothes and bathe frequently. If they do not answer promptly when you phone, you fear that they have died in their sleep or picture them as lying still on the bathroom rug. When your own phone rings you have a sudden fright that it is the police or a hospital clerk calling.

You recall with a start little embarrassing episodes which your parent somehow rationalized; you were only too eager to accept their explanation. Except that occasionally their explanation was a bit too far-fetched, even bizarre or delusional, and you laughed nervously and said, "Oh, Mother!" or "Oh, Daddy!" with perhaps a furtive look around to see if others had heard. About one year before my own mother died she called me on the telephone. After the usual small talk about our health and that of the children, she chilled me with, "I know you're going to laugh at me and say I'm senile, but . . ." She went on to say that she had just bought a quantity of chocolate ice cream which she had put into her freezer. She explained that some of it had been eaten, and who would do a thing like that? "Not I," I responded; "I don't eat chocolate!" "Don't get so smart," said Mother, "I know it wasn't you." "Well, Mother," said I, "you might have eaten it yourself." She denied this vehemently, and I regretted the allegation. "I had just brought it from the store," she insisted in an imperious tone that told me it would be dangerous to pursue this line of questioning. "What do you suppose happened?" I asked, dreading the answer. "Someone could have come in . . ." "To eat your *ice cream*?" "That's all that I noticed. But once they know how to get in . . ."

Well, there's the shocker. Not *once "they" know how to get in*, but once our parents' defenses have crumbled, leaving them vulnerable to nameless terrors, regardless of their source, for which they will supply names, means and motives.

The first crack in the wall does not always mean it will immediately collapse. The masonry of the intellect may shift and the defect fill with the crumbs from adjacent crumblings, but the structure is losing its integrity, and eventually no part will remain to fill in for any other.

Thus we become aware that something will have to be done. Just what, we do not know, so we fear the worst. Yet we don't even have a very clear idea of what "the worst" is! Is it "the worst" for our parent to die outright, or to survive as a vegetable with nurses around the clock, or to move in with us (with or without nurses), or to live in an institution for permanent, final care—the ultimate solution? Which of these *is* the worst?

Often, we don't even know what we fear!

Indeed, the alternatives which we face are few, and the decision essentially makes itself. Unable to continue living alone, our parent will either need someone to move in or will have to live elsewhere with help. And that "someone" will have to be us or someone else. The choice among alternatives will depend on few conditions: our parent's health and our finances, or the community resources available. And, as I have suggested, the decision essentially makes itself, independently of anyone's agonizing. Indeed, our agonizing yields no positive contribution to the decision.

But why are we so upset?

You may wonder if I haven't missed the point! Don't I realize that this is not a simple matter such as deciding whether to go to the mountains or the shore, or what kind of car to buy—that it is an emotional issue rather than an intellectual one? Am I aware that essentially *irrational* forces are at work here, that this isn't just anybody we're talking about, but *our own parent*?

Quite right. You are telling me what we all know: that decisions about aging parents are rarely made objectively, that we can't always do the rational, the practical, the convenient thing, but rather what our heart or conscience will tolerate. I am sure you find in your own experience examples of "what families have put themselves through" in attempting to care for aging parents. You probably know of daughters who have "sacrificed their lives" caring for their mothers, either never marrying or virtually abandoning husbands and children. You know of families who have literally turned a house into a nursing home, assets into debits, and themselves into servants in order to do what they believed to be right and proper.

To all things there is a logic, even to matters of heart and conscience. There must be some sense to what seems to make no sense; even to the nearly total expenditure of home, wealth and self, there is a motive. When directed toward one's parents the motive may sometimes be actual financial profit, as in the instance where one child cares for a parent in order to obtain favored treatment in the parent's will. More commonly, the ultimate explanation for our care of our parents when they can no longer take care of us is not profit, but rather an abstraction such as "love" or "guilt," public opinion, or moral rectitude. To call these explanatory principles "abstractions" is not to suggest that they are not experienced as real; when they dominate, they feel more real than material profit.

But none of these explanations seems really to hit the mark. *Greed* is a familiar and plausible motive and accounts for much human behavior. *Love* is a convenient, readily accessible explanation, but in many cases it lacks credibility simply because of the universality of ambivalence: while we all feel love for our parents, we also feel a degree of anger, resentment and disappointment, occasionally even hate, in our relationship with them. It is embarrassing, if not patently demeaning, to suggest that we take them in out of *guilt*; nowadays it even sounds mildly pathological. *Public opinion* is not to be ignored, and one may add that among the eyes of our beholders are the eyes of our children for whom we are setting an example, for the time when their turn and ours comes. But doesn't this sound somewhat contrived or even manipulative? *Moral rectitude* suggests a sense of righteousness, of alignment with the forces of civilization extending to the Ten Commandments and perhaps beyond; it is the way things are to be done, it is mannerly and orderly, but it does not explain *why* we do it, nor does it reflect what happens on a gut level.

While "all of the above" may be a passing answer, it is neither precise, nor satisfying, nor is *any* of the above adequate payment for the distress we feel as we watch our parents slowly approach death and as we suffer the need to do something for them before the end comes.

To find a better answer we will have to look deeper into our parents and into ourselves. This is necessary because we need to know what we are doing in order to provide meaning for their life and for our own.

Our first consideration will be in terms of what we see. Then we will explore what we feel.

10

You Take A Good Look At Your Parents.

What you see is very disturbing. Are your parents becoming senile?

People grow old in a variety of ways, but the most awesome is when the mind deteriorates. When a parent becomes physically enfeebled it is clear that special care is required. Sometimes it is possible to provide care in their own home or in yours; but a nursing home, by whatever euphemism it masquerades, may be required to provide the technical competence and equipment to maintain the failing organism. However, when the individual is physically intact, but memory and judgment are impaired, there is an extremely difficult decision to be made.

Why is the decision so difficult? There are two kinds of explanations for the difficulty. The first is that the decision is an emotional one, and all emotional decisions are so difficult that we tend to procrastinate, leaving the door open for too many options, or with frantic impulsiveness slam it shut in the face of reason. The second explanation is lack of objective information. One of the reasons for this lack is the emotional fog through which observations are made.

What we need to know, simply and clearly, is the state of our parent's competence. We need to know the kind and amount of assistance that may be required to compensate for the mental abilities that our parent has lost, and thus to make it possible for him or her to survive and enjoy some of life's ordinary pleasures.

To some extent each of our parents, like each one of us, is required to be an executive, at least with respect to the business of staying alive. A certain amount of organizing ability is necessary to deal with the inputs and outputs of daily life, not to mention the requirement for some kind of planning and the need to carry plans through. Even a matter as simple as getting dressed in the morning requires the ability to plan an outfit to wear, so that clothes may be laid out and put on. If we "dress as we go," starting with a randomly selected garment and adding coordinates, the ability to select and reject is necessary. Indeed, if our parent shows up in the morning looking like a patchwork quilt, we are quick to make a critical comment such as, "You look like you got dressed out of a grab bag," or, "Are you going to a hippie convention?" We are too upset to recognize that our parent's organizing ability has been diminished.

Further examples are all too easy to come by, and painful to inventory. Can mother make out a shopping list? Can she find the items in the supermarket? Can father change a light bulb or adjust the thermostat? Is it safe to let them go out or to stay home alone?

For the most part we don't want to know the answers. And when we do know, we'd rather think of other matters. We hope that we won't learn the answers when a parent has an accident at home or on the street.

To organize means simply to keep things in order. When a parent can no longer order his or her daily life, do we not need to bring in another person to assist them? And will the other person be us—or a stranger? And if our parents can no longer be maintained in their own home, will they not have to move to our home or to that of our brother or sister? And will it become necessary to institutionalize our parent?

Does this litany make it all sound ridiculously simple and hardly worth getting excited over? Does it sound very much like the process we go through with our old cars? We make the necessary minor repairs until a major one is needed, and then we wonder whether to make the investment in a new transmission or to get rid of the old heap. If we decide to keep the old bus we are faced with one breakdown after another, toying with the thought that we now have a "classic car" whose value will surely increase. So we keep pouring in money, but along with our classic car we still need reliable transportation. Do we buy a new car (without a trade-in) at this point, or do we get another used car which will soon require major repairs?

The big difference, of course, is that when the problem is with your car, something must be done right away, but when your parent's transmission starts to go you feel free to hope that it is only a temporary aberration and that tomorrow or next week the problem will solve itself. Or else— and honesty requires that we recognize that this possibility exists—it occurs to us that our parent may suddenly and peacefully pass away. Die. But though we think about it we don't care to dwell on it. Because our parents *will* die, and we will also die, and everyone else will die, and there's no hurry to think about it.

Thus we focus on how well our parents are doing, and we talk with them more and more about the old days, which they can remember better than what they had for breakfast, and we remember with them the good times, and they become for us once again young and strong and beautiful and competent. We are able for a moment to reassure ourselves that everything is as it always was, and that when we leave they will still be able to "organize" and to manage their affairs. Except that it isn't so. And this is why we lack the necessary information to plug into the decision-making process. Because essentially we don't want to know, and we don't want to make any decisions except to wait a little longer and see how things develop.

Somewhere along the line you talk to your family doctor, if you're fortunate enough to have a doctor who knows you and your parents and who has the time and patience to sit and talk the situation through. What he will tell you depends on two things. First is his own particular style. He may be the sort of practitioner who gives it to you straight from the shoulder: when you have cancer he tells you the plain truth, and that you'll be dead in six months without surgery, or perhaps you'll live a year with surgery and radiation or chemotherapy. Or he may tell you that he isn't certain, when in fact he is, and that you'll have to go into the hospital for more studies than he can handle in his office. Not that he thinks you have anything serious, but you'd better get this work done just to be on the safe side.

So much for professional style. You know by now whether he's an alarmist or if he was brought up on Dr. Spock. There's still the matter of what he knows about your mother or father. He may have concluded that there is a certain amount of cerebral atherosclerosis ("hardening of the arteries" of the forebrain), but he may have had very little opportunity to observe the behavioral consequences of this illness. For this he is dependent largely on what you are able to tell him about your parent's ability to function, plus what he is able to surmise from your parent's responses.

He may be able to give you good advice and recommend community resources, but he will not be able to tell you how long it will be before your parent will require institutionalization. In no way can he be specific about this.

Various generalizations will emerge from the conversation: It is better for people to stay in their familiar surroundings as long as possible. On the other hand there would not only be more structure but also more stimulation if your parent were with other people. Each choice has its pros and cons.

You may emerge from this meeting reassured, but there is an almost equal probability that you will leave befuddled. In either case the ball is in your court, and there is a good chance that you will resent having to take responsibility for making a decision without sufficient data.

I am not going to tell you how to make the decision about what to do with your parent, and I am in no position to make it for you. The decision will force itself soon enough. But first I would like to explore with you the emotional side of your relationship with your parent. Perhaps there you will be able to unravel a solution to your problem.

11

Do You Really Know Your Own Parents?

You certainly do. You know them in ways you never dreamed of, by mechanisms you never imagined.

What are your parents like? Even after having known them for 30, 40, or 50 years you may not be sure. But it is likely that you know them as well as, or better than, anyone else does. All parents are not the same at the beginning of their careers as parents, and all undergo personality changes as life progresses. You are in the best position to detect these changes and are best able to know when your parents are troubled. This evaluation requires no special clinical training on your part: You become aware of their moods and feelings by direct perception, essentially by intuition. Another way of putting this is to say that you feel it in your insides; you have a visceral response to your parents' visceral reactions (emotions). When your parents are upset, you are upset.

When you were growing up at home the impact of your parents' moods was enormous. Their fears, anger and in-

securities would tear at you, at times making you feel
physically ill. As you matured and established your own
home you were able to escape somewhat from the influence of their inner feelings, but even if you were living
apart from them a visit or a telephone call might generate
the same old gut reactions. Sometimes it might seem that
they were deliberately manipulating your physiology with
an eery parental power, and at times this may have been
close to the truth. But more commonly they were simply
being themselves on a particular day—perhaps even trying to spare you pain, but unable to do so because of the
invisible connection between their feelings and yours
which persisted after the umbilical cord was cut.

And so you do know how they feel, perhaps better than
you ever cared to know.

This visceral response, the feeling of connection, has
probably been a source of discomfort, but seen in another
way, it can be considered not only as a source of pain, but
rather as a source of information: the way they make *you*
feel tells you something important about the way *they* feel.

I would like to emphasize here that I am not talking
about *sympathy*, but rather about *empathy*. Sympathy is a
kindly or tender feeling that one person has for another
whom he recognizes as being in a difficult plight. It is
based on awareness and understanding. Empathy is a more
direct, primitive, nonintellectual sharing of an emotional
response in the absence of the protective barriers which
normally separate us from each other.

We don't learn anything about the other person when we
feel sympathy for him, but empathy reveals the other's
inner self.

It is on this basis that we know that our parents are
troubled.

*   *   *

It's startling, isn't it, to know that what we feel is what they feel?

To put it in a slightly different way: it's only because they feel it in themselves that we feel it in ourselves. If everything were going well with our parents—if they were healthy, comfortable, confident—would we be developing a sense of insecurity? In ordinary parlance, the sense of insecurity is "about" our parents: We feel uneasy "about" them. I am now saying that the insecurity comes *from* the parents, that it is directly communicated from them to us. Even when they try to keep it from us, they are letting us know that they are in pain, or frightened, or worried.

I don't believe that parents are simply being manipulative or "doing a number on us" when they say it's all right if we don't come over for dinner, that they'll just have a bowl of soup or a piece of bread and cheese and go to bed early. This may produce in us a little gastrointestinal twinge which we learn to call "guilt," but it is not correct to say that parents do it in order to make us feel guilty. Our old mother is thinking, "Well, if they don't come over for dinner, I'll just heat a can of soup, or I'll have some bread and finish some leftovers from the refrigerator." She is also feeling bad that we are not coming, and our visceral response is the direct perception of her disappointment.

Mother does not need to manipulate now; the direct connection between our emotions, between our guts, was established in our infancy, some of it, indeed, while we were in her womb, where we had ample opportunity to learn what was going on in her insides. And after we were born, after our guts had learned to follow hers, we learned to associate words, movements and expressions with the internal manifestations of emotion. So the "manipulation" is programmed. Mother is "not guilty."

While mother may be innocent of deliberate manipulation, there *is* a sense in which she is guilty. After all, if she had not felt disappointed at our not coming for dinner, we would not have felt the twinge that we interpreted as feelings of guilt! Let me now raise a question and suggest an answer. Why did mother have to feel disappointed? And the answer is: Because she is not a computer. On the basis of our coming to dinner in the past, a computer would have developed a probabilistic statement describing the number of chances in 100 that we would appear. This would be analogous to mother's "expectation" that we would come. If we did *not* come, however, the computer would change the odds, but it wouldn't get emotional; mother, on the other hand, whether or not she had ever studied statistics, would be most likely to feel disappointed, even though she knew there were many reasons why we might not come, and even though she might remember precisely the number of times we had "disappointed" her in the past ten years.

With mother it's all or nothing. You love me or you don't love me. And if we don't show up, we don't love her! The subsequent steps are absolutely predictable:

1. Well, they have their own lives to lead.
2. But they could find time for me.
3. What selfish children!
4. Where did I go wrong?
5. Maybe I wasn't a good mother.

These steps occur in less time than they take to write about or read. And mother's disappointment is *almost* concurrent with her guilt feelings at not having been a good mother. There is an instant at the beginning of the disappointment when she feels angry (which doesn't bother us, because we too feel angry, only we perceive it as self-righteousness), but as soon as the guilt phase begins, we perceive it directly as guilt. Only we perceive it as our guilt, not realizing it's identical with hers.

*   *   *

Not that we want to minimize the anger. Some parents are more angry than others, and even those of us who aren't usually angry can occasionally become enraged. As children we correctly fear our parents' anger. But it is inappropriate for this fear to continue into our own middle age, and it should properly be called neurotic, that is, out of place. If in middle age we continue to fear the loss of our parents' love, we are in trouble! While most people get over this kind of fear, very many don't. The healthy way to respond to anger is reciprocal anger: such transactions have the most favorable outcome for both participants, because no one ends up one-up or one-down, and the matter can come to a reasonable conclusion. Accordingly, when mother goes through steps 1, 2, and 3, we have a right to get into "Well, we *do* have our own lives to lead, and our presence at the committee meeting (or whatever) is important to us and to the committee."

Our anger is reactive, the response of one ego when banged by another. You hit me, I hurt; I hurt, I yell.

But our guilt responding to her guilt is not up front like our anger responding to her anger. It is uncanny, resonating to the eery vibrations of an electronic oscillator. It is the result of conditioning in our infancy, or even earlier, when we were yet unborn.

12

You Must Acknowledge
Mixed Emotions.

*Mingled with your love for your parents you find
areas of resentment.*

Possibly the reader may be thinking, "Isn't this what
always happens when you get involved with a psychiatrist? He wants to go all the way back to your childhood!
And this one is even worse: He wants to go back to before
you were born!"

Well, in order to get a good running start before leaping I
thought we'd go back to your adolescence, and then I
decided to go back to your parents' adolescence. I want to
be free to go back as far as may be required to make my
points understandable. But, not to worry; you will note
that this book has a back cover, so the analysis must come
to an end!

I have a good reason for wanting to return to your adolescence: that was the time when you began to assert your
independence from your parents in a positive way, that is,
by demonstrating your ability to deal with the world in a
way that would lead to mature adulthood. I refer not only

to choosing a vocation and becoming absorbed in the process of preparing for a career. While there is certainly no way in which you can become a mature adult without both relationships *and* vocation, what I had in mind was something a little more ambitious: the beginnings of a world view, a sense of your place in home, school, community, history, universe. Not as a meaningless piece of space junk, but as an effective being.

I am stressing the adaptive aspects of independence, because all of us learn a kind of negative independence very early in life. At age two we learn to say "no" and to knock over our strained spinach; not many years later we learn to lie and cheat, and to hit people from their blind side. And eventually we learn to become rebellious (and even tediously repetitious), all of which are signs of a certain kind of independence, but not exactly what I had in mind.

I am not suggesting that somewhere between the ages of sixteen and twenty-five you actually wrote out a personal philosophy, or even that you brought one into reflective consciousness. Not everyone is inclined to conceptual thought. Many of us "think" best in forms of sound, movements, color, or in completed acts, or in their organization. This is why some painters are unable to tell us in words what they are saying on canvas, letting the picture speak for itself. Similarly, very successful investors may never produce a coherent dissertation on how they select their stocks. (Of course they may not want to do so.)*

The development of a sense of *self* and of *place* (i.e., the sense that your self has a place, that it belongs somewhere) is significant not merely in career or vocation, but in your entire lifestyle, in your own family life—whether or not you are monogamous, marry, have children, your use of hobbies, sports, travel, food, home repairs, and whether or not you like to make lists.

---

*One reasonably successful investor told me, "I have good taste."

Adolescence, of course, is a time of crisis, not necessarily that yours was a stormy period, but nevertheless a time of crisis in that you struggled with the issue of whether to adopt your parents' ways, or to develop a lifestyle of your own.

At this stage of my exposition I need your help because I am going to propose some points with which you may or may not agree. These points are more or less indigenous to psychiatric thinking, and some of my patients complain that this kind of reasoning is self-serving, that it creates a no-win situation for them and a no-lose one for me (though I don't see how the patient loses if the psychiatrist is right). Since you didn't come to me for treatment, and have no more to lose than a couple of hours and the cost of this book, you may not see any problem here.

The points are:

1. The extent to which adolescence is a time of crisis is mainly a function of the kind of parenting the adolescent has received up to that point. (It's hard to disagree with this unless you believe that 51 percent of the variance may be accounted for by peer pressure and immeasurables. Anyway, this point isn't crucial.)
2. The lifestyle adopted by the adolescent moving into adulthood mainly either conforms with a parental lifestyle or is a reaction against it.
3. In the process of conforming with or rejecting a parental lifestyle, certain expectations are built up in the adolescent or young adult's mind which, if unfulfilled, lead either to feelings of resentment or feelings of guilt, or both, toward his or her parents.

What seems to bother some individuals is the either/or aspect of Point Two: that no matter what you do, you're either going along with your parents or you're reacting against them. It may be difficult to substantiate either horn of this dilemma, but I think that the alternative position— that your course is unrelated to that of your parents—

would be even more difficult to prove. Furthermore, it wouldn't matter one way or the other if not for Point Three: the feelings of resentment and/or guilt resulting from the failure of your expectations to materialize.

There is an old saying that we usually take credit for our successes and blame others for our failures. If we are extremely generous, or if we should win an Academy Award, we may be able to acknowledge how much others have helped us. But if we fail, is it not human nature to find excuses and to put the onus on another's shoulders? And if our whole life is a bust, whom do we blame? Who else but good old Mom and Dad, the two most deserving people we know! Here's how it works.

Back to the point of adolescent choice. In retrospect, it's striking how little flexibility there is in life for most of us. Unless we make the right moves at the right time we soon find ourselves locked in, and if we have made the wrong choice at a crucial juncture we are confronted with frustration and failure. The successful gamesman makes moves which offer the greatest number of options of the best quality. But in adolescence how many of us know this rule, or knowing it, can choose which moves to make? How many of us have the benefit of very good advice?

But good or not, there usually is a surplus of advice available, and parents are the major source of this input. Parents commonly claim to "know" what it is that we should be doing with our life, and they usually feel that it is appropriate to pass these insights on to us. Even the more reserved parents communicate by example, and there is an implicit message that their example should set a pattern for all future human behavior, especially yours.

Having been given the word, the future lies before us with the mathematical clarity of Boulean algebra, as we proceed along the diverging branches of a logic tree, beneath whose boughs we will ultimately come to rest. In a sense it may be better to be down a tree than up one, but as I see it, there is little to choose either way, and as we shall learn directly, the outcome of the first round of play is based strictly on dumb luck, unless one is able to take pride in how cleverly he has chosen his ancestors.

For we shall either follow our parents' advice, or model, or we shall not. They in their wisdom, may encourage us to become either a cop or a robber. You may protest that no proper parent will teach his child to be a crook, but I can think immediately of two cases in which he (or she) does just that: when the parent is a successful crook, and when the parent is a scrupulously honest failure, and whose consequent behavior reflects a bitter recrimination.

Whether you accept this proposition or not, let me return to my logic tree. If the parent encourages the child to become a minion of the law, the child may either follow the parent's explicit wish and become part of the justice system (i.e., policeman, lawyer) or choose an allied vocation (teacher, clergyman), or he or she may opt for an illegal or dishonest occupation. If he enters the justice system, he may become an honest cop or a crooked cop, and in either case he may become successful or unsuccessful.

Put succinctly, he will do what his parents want him to do or he will do the opposite. And in either case he will become a success or a failure. The odds are one in four, then, that he will both follow his parents' wishes *and* be successful at what he does. There is also one chance in four that he will oppose them and nevertheless be successful, and there are two chances in four that he will not be successful whether he follows or opposes. (Of course these odds are only for the logical categories; the exact probability of each is a matter for empirical test.)

Our concern, of course, is not with the mathematics of the breakdown, but with the psychological consequences of each: in each case, how does the child end up feeling about his parent? Let's say, for the sake of the argument, that your father or your mother is a lawyer and wants you to become a lawyer, and you do. All goes well, and you're reasonably successful at the law. How do you feel toward your parent? Other things being equal, you should have a quite positive feeling. This is a happy outcome, and I, for one, would be quite content if life always worked out this way, but of course it can't and it doesn't. We live in a vertically mobile society, and there is not always good correlation between parental occupation and that of the offspring. Your father may be a tailor and want you to be a doctor, or you may have no father, and your mother may want you to become a teacher. So a smooth continuity of life with fortuitous outcomes is not likely to be commonplace.

Furthermore, we all know perfectly well that a child may follow the course laid down by a parent, be successful at it, and nevertheless spend the rest of his life brooding with some vague discomfort or feeling of outright anger at the parent or himself for not having shown more independence or initiative. There is, indeed, a good chance that he will be happier with himself and with his parents, if he charts his own course.

However, there is a notable difference between charting your own course and doing the opposite of what a parent wants. To be simplistic again, if your parent wants you to become a cop and you become a robber, the compulsive reaction in doing the opposite of what Simon Says is hardly a free choice.

In any event, there's something very satisfying about being successful, and it carries with it the implication that someone did something right, and that one's parents can't be such bad people after all.

But, on the other hand, suppose you didn't make out so well? Why then, it is obviously your parents' fault. If you followed their wishes and became what they wanted you to become, wasn't there an implied promise to you that you would be successful, indeed that you would be happy?

And if things didn't go well, doesn't that mean that they broke their promise and are no longer deserving of your love and respect?

And even if you didn't follow them, instead went your own way, and it didn't work out very well, shouldn't they have stopped you and gotten you back on track before it was too late? Shouldn't they have gotten you off to a fresh start and seen to it that everything went all right?

And even though your head may answer no, your heart will always say *yes*.

13

No Wonder. They Made You What You Are Today.

No matter how independent you may feel, the influence of your parents has been uncanny.

We middle-aged types who read and write books such as this one tend to be so preoccupied with success that it becomes the heartbeat of our lives, with any deviation from the norm uneasily noted. I am talking specifically about *getting ahead* to whatever goal we identify as "success" regardless of whether it fits with the pattern of achievement laid down for us by our parents. This kind of success is characterized by one's position or status, and includes financial security.

There is another kind of success that might be termed a successful lifestyle. I would not contend that there is no relationship between being a success and having a successful lifestyle, but one does not necessarily follow from the other. By a successful lifestyle I mean the way we behave when we feel good about ourselves: comfortable, confident. To be sure, one of the bases for feeling that way is having achieved material, professional or political success. But you can feel good about yourself simply because of the way you handle your own body and the objects around you, and because of the way you relate to your environment, especially to other people. This is another way of saying that you will feel good about yourself if you are physically and mentally healthy.

In the previous chapter I proposed that in our search for material success, we follow the life course recommended by our dominant parent (i.e., the "spokesparent"), or else we oppose it. While I would scarcely call this a choice, at least there are alternatives. But when it is a matter of lifestyle, specifically as it derives from the way we feel about ourselves, I hold that there is neither choice nor alternative, and that it is all laid out in a mother's love.

Yes, this woman, your mother, who may now be becoming senile, whose life is in your hands, was the principal determinant of your lifestyle. If she loved you, you feel beloved, and therefore you feel good about yourself. But if she did not love you, you feel unworthy of love and incapable of developing a successful lifestyle based on ease and self-confidence. You are not comfortable within your own skin and cannot be confident in your dealings beyond it.

It should come as no surprise that mothers are not always able to love their own children. Not to love does not necessarily mean to neglect or to abuse (indeed it may lead to overprotectiveness!), but it does mean to deprive a son or a daughter of warmth, security, trust, faith, and hope. On the positive side it produces meanness, pettiness, nastiness, bitterness, stinginess, cynicism and a tendency to be annoyingly self-righteous. (I am of the opinion that cheating is a result of maternal overprotectiveness, but some adored babies grow up to cheat because it has never occurred to them that they might lose at anything. Fathers have a part in this, too, especially with respect to defining the limits imposed by the real world.)

There are many reasons why mothers may not love their babies. First would be an unreadiness for motherhood, in the sense of not yet having lived through their own childhood or adolescence: when a woman is still a girl emotionally, any pregnancy is an unwanted pregnancy, and any child an unwanted child. And a disastrously difficult pregnancy may make it difficult for the mother to love the product of that pregnancy, though she may instead take out her annoyance on her mate, her own mother, or even on her doctor.

But I believe that the main reason why a mother fails to love her baby is because it doesn't feel right to her, because the actual physical contact with the baby is not pleasurable—as when an adult hugs another adult while knowing that love is not possible. Doubtless there are some mothers who could love any baby, just as there may be some women who could love any man, but most humans are not so universal in their adaptiveness. Some women, by choice or fate, seem able to go to bed with any man, but that is not the same as loving the partner. A prostitute is not devoid of preferences, and most women are very particular about whom they will accept as lovers, even more so with respect to selecting a mate and father for their children. (Yes, I know that men can go to bed with any woman, but they can't always perform with any woman.)

But there are a variety of reasons why women marry whom they do, and love may not always be the overriding consideration. Thus it follows that a woman may have a child by a man she does not really love, a man whose body does not even feel good to her, even though he may believe that she feels very good to him. (After all, what do men know?)

Accordingly, there is a significant statistical probability that one of the children a woman has by a man she doesn't love will feel no better to her than did his father (I say "his," but this ill-starred child might well be a daughter). Beginning with an incompatibility of texture or of motility (doubtless certain hyperactive babies would be included here), or even of unconsciously perceived odor, not knowing *what* is wrong but knowing that *something* is wrong, the mother will come to perceive in the child qualities of the unloved father and will transfer to the child the unexpressed resentment she has held toward the husband she does not love. And when we begin to speak of the transfer of feelings, it will have to be acknowledged that, once a baby does not feel quite right to the mother, she may project on to it negative feelings originating from almost any source. The baby may become a target for mother-hate deriving from the mother's own mother or father. Once things start to go wrong, Murphy's Law* comes inexorably into play.

Having painted this gloomy picture, I do not recommend that you immediately jump off a bridge. But if you don't love your mother you're in enough trouble already without feeling guilty about it; there may be a very good reason for it: perhaps she didn't love you.

By now I realize that I may have committed the ultimate sin: I may have attacked your own mother. As a consequence of this you may be angry with me, but it's all right: I'm used to it. I understand that it's *my fault* for telling you. It's not my fault that your mother didn't love you (if she didn't), and it's not my fault for your resenting your mother (if you do), for not loving you (if she didn't); it's merely my fault for *telling* you about it. The person you should be angry with if your mother didn't love you is your *father*, because he failed to make her happy. (It's probably not really his fault either, but we needn't go into that.)

---

*Anything that can go wrong probably will.

*   *   *

Let's go back to where I said it was your father's responsibility to make your mother love you. How was he to have accomplished this? In only one way: by making your mother happy. Indeed, as far as you were concerned, your father had only one responsibility: to keep your mother happy. If he did this she loved you. Whatever else he may or may not have accomplished—whether he was President of the United States or on welfare—mattered only to the extent to which it made your mother happy or unhappy.

It is necessary to be clear about this. Making your mother happy does not mean that he was obligated to give her her own way in all things. In large measure it means to have kept her feeling loved, sexually happy, fulfilled as a woman. Her material or career ambitions were only secondarily important. If they appeared to be primary, it was because your father was not keeping her happy in the ways he might have.

Of course there are complications. It may be that your mother brought such severe emotional problems into the marriage that your father was unable to deal with them. It is completely unreasonable to expect either spouse to make up for deficiencies in his or her in-laws (in-law jokes are no joke!). All that your father could have done in such a case was to straighten himself out (alone or with help) as best he could and secured the best available professional help for your mother.

Now the reason I say that as far as you are concerned your father's only job was to make your mother happy is that her only job was to love you. I will now proceed to tell you very succinctly, and I hope clearly, why I believe this.

There are, fortunately, only two cases that we have to consider, since everyone is either a son or a daughter. (I say "fortunately" because the explication of this matter will sound simultaneously very simple and very complex.) First, consider the case of the son.

We have already established that a man's feeling of self-worth depends on his mother's love. There is here a great possibility for what would appear to be error: a man may accomplish very little in his life and nevertheless feel absolutely great—simply because his mother loved him! On the other hand, why should that trouble us? Are we his judge, jury, moral sense? No. This is not a problem for anyone—anyone except his wife. There is a good chance that a man who feels loved by his mother may feel loved by the universe without his having raised a finger to deserve it. This would make him satisfied with himself, but he would not be likely to be the sort of man who would make his wife happy. Accordingly, none of us would want him for a father. Why? Because our mother would be unhappy and not free in her heart to pour feelings of love into us. Indeed, she might become such a nagging wife that her husband might self-righteously indicate that the source of all the family problems is mother's nagging, thus obscuring the fact that she is nagging only because of his inability to give love to her. In the face of such a standoff the mother may turn away from her husband and pour an overprotecting love into her son. This would make him feel loved, but the love would have a hook in it: an awful sense of responsibility and premature seriousness.

But if father loves mother, then mother can love her son appropriately, not requiring from him any of the kind of support a mother properly expects only from her husband. The boy, getting only what he should get from his mother, does not have to feel guilty toward, and afraid of, his father. Thus the entire Oedipal conflict* situation need not develop. Indeed what *does* happen is that the son, not hat-

---

*Yes, I'm saying what you think I'm saying. The Oedipus complex is not a normal phase in development, but is rather the pathological consequence of fathers and mothers not understanding their role in the family.

ing or fearing his father, is then able to have strong positive feelings toward his father, whom he identifies with and strives to emulate.

The second case is that of the daughter. If father doesn't love mother, he may pour too much love into his daughter, and she, like brother with mother, may be quite confused as to what is expected of her. Indeed, father may consciously or unconsciously have sexual expectations of his daughter, of which she will be consciously or unconsciously aware, with overt or covert consequences. This may lead to seductiveness, sexual abuse, or the familiar Electra Complex, which is no more normal than is the Oedipus Complex in boys. When I say "not normal" I don't mean uncommon. Sinus trouble and arthritis are common enough, but they're not normal conditions. On the other hand, if father loves mother, daughter *sees* it, *feels* it, and, free of inappropriate feelings toward her father, need not feel guilty toward her mother, freeing her to identify with and emulate mother, and to proceed along the way to becoming a woman.

The fortunate sons and daughters whose fathers love their mothers, and whose mothers are able to respond, may or may not achieve material success, but they will certainly have a successful lifestyle. Their chances for happiness are good.

PART III

Worse News: Not Only Are Your Parents Getting Old, *You* Will Grow Old!

Part of the problem of thinking about what to do with your aging parents is that you don't like to think about aging at all!

14

Must Everyone Become Senile?

Is senility in your genes—or is there something you can do to keep from becoming dotty?

One of the things that bothers us most about old people is that they seem lost. They don't know what to do with themselves and are in constant need of amusement, which, when provided, often seems not to prove very entertaining. They seem not to be in touch with what's going on, they don't get the joke, they show no interest, they forget the beginning of the story before they get to the end of it. There isn't anything they really want to do, and we tend to assume that they expect us to invent a program of activities for them. It isn't necessarily true that they have such an expectation of us, but we think or feel that they do, and we become disturbed and behave as though we were trying to do something about it. We find we are not very successful, and this frustrates us further.

There are two principal reasons for the apparent apathy of elderly parents. The first and most obvious of these is biological, senility itself: irreversible damage to the brain. The second is a common illness that is usually reversible:

depression. In addition to being sad and sometimes agitated, people who are depressed are frequently slowed in their activity, their sleeping and eating patterns are altered, and they lose interest in almost everything, including sex, although they may maintain an obsessive pseudo-interest in a particular idea, usually one that makes them appear in an unfavorable light, or that makes them express feelings of guilt.

When the psychiatrist is successful in treating the depression there commonly remains brain damage which we are powerless to do much about. Of course, doctors may prescribe vitamins and various nutritional substances, as well as drugs, that theoretically should improve the blood supply to the brain, but none of these medications is able to restore the function of brain cells that are dead and have been replaced by deposits of fat and obstinate connective tissue. From time to time people with senile brain deterioration do appear brighter and more alert, but these apparent improvements are temporary, for the course is predictably downhill. "Good days and bad days" are especially characteristic of people who have cerebral atherosclerosis, and may be related to variations in blood flow and fluid balance.

It is true that even old brains can learn new tricks, so it is obviously desirable to maintain optimal functioning in the aged. Therefore it is important and necessary to treat depression in old age, and to maintain the best possible physical health.

All of this may seem rather gloomy, but there is one aspect of the aging process that is hopeful, to which I will devote the remainder of this book, and to which society should devote a major effort. I am not suggesting that medical research into the biological process of aging should be neglected—indeed it must receive increasing support—in favor of what I am about to propose. Both efforts should be carried on simultaneously.

As people grow old they appear to undergo various personality changes. What we see in them, however, does not represent something new and different. If we observe carefully we see that the apparent personality changes are actually exaggerations of previously existing personality characteristics. People become what they have always been, only more so. The thrust of this observation is to focus attention on the pre-senile personality, what an individual was like before he or she grew old.

The most general concept that I have to propose is that what one is like when one is old is significantly determined by how one lives one's life. This statement is sufficiently self-evident and I suspect it will be generally acceptable, which encourages me to go on to the next statement, which I believe follows logically: There is a way to live one's life that can reduce the ravages of senility.

My second proposition is not much different from my first, but rephrasing it opens up a world of possibilities. One may now ask, "Is there actually a way that I, as an adult, can live, so that when I am old I can continue to think young and maintain interest in the world and in my own life?" I believe that this is the case, and while I certainly am not going to tell you how to live your life, there are certain principles that are worth considering.

There is much talk these days about being "reborn" or "born again," particularly with regard to religious conversion. In his *Varieties of Religious Experience*, first published in 1902, William James wrote of the "once born" and the "twice born." The once born are those born with faith, which they retain; the twice born grew up without faith, or had it and lost it, and then had a profound religious experience or conversion.

There is another sense in which one can be once born or twice born: with respect to what, for want of a better term, I will call "track," in the sense in which one can be "on track" or "off track." I'm not talking about betting on horses, but about one's own life track. This relates to the concept of *vocation*, but it is equally related to *avocation*, and must inevitably touch on such areas as identity, integrity of the ego, and self-realization or actualization, and most especially authenticity and good faith. But it is probably just as clear to speak of finding one's own track and staying on it, as it is to utilize more specialized terminology.

It is a good and wondrous thing to find one's own track and to stay on it! Most of us never quite make it. During our middle teen years, some intimation of a track, like the meaning of an obscure poem, suggests the possibility of an intersect between reality and the unconscious mind, the corner of Fifth and Tenth Avenues, the conjunction of Hollywood and Wilshire Boulevards. Short of infinity, the parallels converge, but with other names: Hollywood and Vine, Broadway and 42nd Street. Whimsy makes its bow to reality, and the process of accommodation is under way.

Everyone must make compromises or accommodations. Indeed, it may be possible to define maturity, sophistication or diplomacy as the ability to adapt. Someone defined politics as "the art of the possible" (and I sometimes apply the same definition to psychiatry). On the other hand, from a certain perspective, we often have unflattering things to say about compromisers and people who are able to make accommodations, especially in "compromising" situations. In an earlier time we were taught to believe that it is important to be men and women of *principle*, and that wily European negotiators were unethical and amoral. Nowadays, of course, it is common knowledge that the methods ascribed to Machiavelli and Metternich are standard operating procedure, and that anyone who tells you exactly where he stands is naive and potentially a loser.

But of course I am speaking only of the short run. We do what we can to win a contract, get a treaty signed or get elected. Contracts, however, are usually of brief duration, treaties are commonly terminated unilaterally, and terms in office self-limiting. But adult life and old age go on for the long run, and unless we know who we are and what we stand for, we will in our later years suffer the consequences.

15

Keeping On Your Life Track.

If you stay on the right track, you may be able to resist senility. But as a young adult you may already have made the wrong turn.

The concept of the Adolescent Moratorium is now reasonably well established in our culture, based on the writings of Eric H. Erickson. Erickson didn't invent the adolescent moratorium, but he was the first to define it. The idea is that, at least in our society, we have the phenomenon of boys and girls who are past puberty with nothing important to do except to hang around and spend money, and possibly get into trouble. No real work is required of them apart from going to school and preparing for a lifelong career. We know that adolescence begins with puberty, but we don't have a definite point where it ends, except that it ends when one becomes an adult. This period is termed a "moratorium" because society could demand that teenagers get to work and start developing their adult lives immediately, but does not do so. Indeed, our society not only doesn't demand that youth get to work, but often has little to offer them if they want to quit school and find a job, or if their family situation requires them to earn money.

83

The term "moratorium," which essentially means a "postponement," suggests that by deferring its demand for productive work, society is doing the adolescent a favor. Inasmuch as adolescents are not all alike, it is likely that they are not uniformly benefited by a moratorium. Certainly there are some who have a tendency to ruminate, to worry about their physical development and about the apparent terrors of adult responsibility, and who would be well served by a well structured program that would sweep them gently but firmly into the mainstream of industrial or professional life. Many adolescents are probably better off without this, and are strengthened by a gradual process of familiarization with their changing emotional and physical selves, and by learning how they fit into the reality of social life. In this process they formulate ideals about how life should be lived and how society should be structured while dreaming of how wonderful life could be if only this or that were true.

Adolescents are usually reminded by adults that their plans are vague and unrealistic, and that they will end up losers or worse unless they get some sense into their heads. As time goes on the harried adolescents most often do become more stable as they grow more familiar with their own selves and the world around them. Plans get sharper and goals look more plausible. The possibility of a major breakthrough in human relationships and of getting in touch with the universe seem almost within reach. Just a little more effort, and all will be well.

But a funny thing happens on the way to Nirvana. Suddenly the adolescent is no longer an adolescent, he or she has become a young adult. Formal education has come to an end. Parents announce that the supply line has been cut: the time has come to make it alone.

The dreams are interrupted, the plans abandoned. There follows a job as an accountant, a salesman, an engineer, a junior executive; perhaps professional school; then marriage. The Better World will have to wait. It's time to settle down and get into the mainstream.

But what has happened to the dreams and the plans and the ideals? They will have to be tabled, set aside, postponed. The former adolescent has now entered the Adult Moratorium, relieved of the awesome responsibility of creating a Better World. All that remains to do now is to work, raise a family, step on someone's neck and get ahead. The easy stuff, programmed into his primitive, archaic "reptilian" brain, that only asks, like a frog, do I eat it or does it eat me?

Thus, both the adolescent and the adult may be said to enjoy a moratorium. The adolescent does not have to worry about supporting a family, while the adult doesn't have to worry about saving the world through love. Clearly it is from the adult point of view that the adolescent experiences a moratorium, but from whose point of view is the adult similarly favored? Certainly not from the adult vantage point. Just try to tell the average adult that he has been blessed and is now passing through a period of deferred responsibility! He or she might respond with sarcastic queries such as, You mean I don't have to pay my taxes and mortgage this month? Or, I can stop worrying about my kids? Or, the ulcer in my stomach is really all in my head?

Like many pronouncements by "experts," the concept of the Adult Moratorium can be made to sound esoteric or even silly when viewed in the context of daily living. But when "something happens" to us or to a member of our family, or to one of our friends or contemporaries (and I don't mean something good, but rather something bad, like a heart attack), suddenly we begin to wonder about matters usually beyond our immediate concern: What is life all about? What am I here for? What is really important? Our concerns imperceptibly pass beyond energy crises, nuclear threats, and international exchange, to the crises of existence, to threats of our impending dissolution, and to the exchange of our material state for a spiritual one, or for a state of non-being, depending on our notions about death.

It is not difficult to see similarities between the concerns of the adolescent and those of the adult moving into middle age. Both, for different reasons, are more than ordinarily conscious of their own mortality; they think more often about death than children or young adults do, and possibly more than—or in a different way from—old people, who are confronted with imminent death. Paradoxically, adolescent concern with death arises from growth forces, from pubertal changes which are being integrated with the old body as a new one is formed. The biological reproductive urges which are a source of excitement and joy, resonate with a deep and aboriginal pattern programmed into the nucleotides of the genetic substance, introducing in the manner of the first movement of a symphony the happy themes of birth and growth, but also the somber and chilling themes of decay and death. Perhaps this is why brides and others cry at weddings.

The reason why middle-aged people think about death is scarcely worth belaboring here. In the midst of one's maximum power and effectiveness, some part, some organ system, begins to work poorly, and that's enough to reintroduce the death theme. Another way to see the Adult Moratorium is as a respite from concern about death. There are some thirty years (or as few as twenty, or as many as forty) when our main concern is to go about the business of *living* without having to worry about *dying*. These are the years when we're raising our children. (Presumably, if we thought about death all the time we might not have any children. Thus the Adult Moratorium may be the means of preserving the species.)

16

It's All Right To Think About Death.

To get back on track you'll have to do some long-range planning. Don't be afraid to plan for your own death.

Over the years I have met very few people who—regardless of religious affiliation—maintain a simple faith in an afterlife. Not knowing what is to be, and having become attached to what is, few are willing to give up the known for the unknown, unless one is suffering great physical or mental anguish. Death, for most, is the adversary of life.

Thought of in this way, death is our great competitor in a zero sum game: if he wins we lose, and as long as we win, death loses. Score a plus for winning and a minus for losing, add them together and you get a zero sum game.

On the other hand, if we and death are on the *same* side, it is impossible for *either* to lose, and we end up with two big pluses. I realize that when it is all over, we are just as dead, but there *is* a difference. The difference appears in how we live, which necessarily includes how we die, since dying is a part of living, not a part of being dead.

The major advantage of being on the same side as death is that it enables us to banish fear (since death is now on our side), and it also enables us to think about death (who is our colleague, and our teamwork will be better if we think about him, as when we play doubles in tennis).

Ordinarily (in the zero sum game) we don't think about death. Indeed we very much make a point of *not* thinking about death. We don't want to let him know that we're thinking about him because if he found out, it would give him some kind of advantage. He would "hear" us thinking about him and then he would know where we are. Neither do we want to hide from him, for he would hear the rustle of our clothing as we try to slip away. So we walk straight ahead, as through a dangerous part of town, looking neither to the right nor to the left, with resolute step, as though we knew where we were going and were expected.

This kind of hide-and-seek behavior of course goes back to our childhood, not merely back to playing with our peers, but back to hiding (ourselves or something we had done) from our parents. It often seems that we have a kind of sneaky, guilty relationship with death, as though our having been born was an affront to him and our continued survival a taunt.

To put this in a more direct form: if one is in hiding, afraid to think about death or dying, it's also true that one is afraid to think about life.

It is not only those "in hiding" who keep a low profile, who fear death. Some of our most energetic, flamboyant citizens—people of whom we say, "They live as though there's no tomorrow"—are so terrified of death that they rush madly into life, gobbling it up before they are in turn consumed.

And there are always critics available to remind over-achievers, "You can't take it with you." All one needs, after all, is a single gold coin to pay Charon for the ferry ride across the Styx.

Indeed there are many forms that the denial of death may take. Whether we "lie low" so that death won't see us or "fly high" as though he isn't there at all, the principle is the same: we simply aren't being realistic. Dying is a part of life, and we do well to plan and organize our life with this in mind.

I contend that there is a way to live "for your whole life" in an integrated way, including, of course, the way you handle your old age.

If all of the preceding sounds like a sales pitch for estate planning, let me assure you that it's not, nor am I selling shares in a retirement community. Neither am I starting a new church. I am proposing that you develop a way of thinking about life and death that will bring unity to adolescence, adulthood and old age.

In order to achieve this, certain obstacles must be overcome. These differ in each stage of life, yet basically they are alike. For the adolescent, the obstacle lies in accepting the inevitability of adult reality. For the adult it is the inevitability of old age. For the old it is—not the inevitability—but the *elusiveness* of death, as well as life. Nothing is firmly in our grasp. And in this way the three stages are alike: we can't hang on to what we have, nor can we get a grip on the next stage of existence (or non-existence, as the case may be).

In my opinion, the key to achieving pervital unity (*pervital*: throughout one's life) may be found in the adolescent conflict. The adolescent is fascinated with death because he fears life. And the reason the adolescent fears life is because he is afraid that in the process of becoming an adult he will have to relinquish everything he holds dear.

Adolescence is an impassioned period. The objects of adolescent passion are not unfamiliar: love, sex, food (especially junk food), and above all, it would seem, recording groups. The objects themselves are not accidental, for love, music, sex, and food are not random choices, but represent universal values. They occupy a common space in that they are all life-related. Yet I have failed to include other adolescent passions, such as death and drugs, which are by definition life-avoiding. Nor have I included religion, which subtends all others.

As I have called the adolescent "impassioned," he or she might also be called "religious." Not necessarily in a formal sense, but religious in the sense of being fervent, and fervently seeking an object for the fervor: some place to put faith. "Faith" is the adolescent's conjugant, an attachment to the universe, a way to find a way of belonging. For, after all, the main business of an adolescent is to accomplish the transition from being child in one's family to becoming an adult in the world.

From the point of view of most adults, of course, the way into the adult world is by acquiring a trade, skill, profession, finding a job, arbitrarily if need be, but in any event by storming the citadel of Reality, or by entering it by stealth, through connections, or if necessary by bribery. But certainly to break in one way or another, and to avoid being left out in the cold.

Thus the alienation of the adolescent. To do, to become, without loving or without faith, is not the rape of the universe, but the rape of the self, of the spirit. This kind of thinking or feeling to the adult is an indulgence in romanticism, hence the failure in communication between the generations.

If it were possible to be neither an adolescent nor an adult (and similarly neither a child nor senile), while maintaining a curiosity about the generational conflict, we could recognize the validity as well as the hypocrisy in both positions. Unfortunately for the cause of objectivity, we all tend to be on one side or the other, and are accordingly distressed to be told that the dross of hypocrisy is mixed with the pure gold of our righteousness.

"Hypocrisy" is a harsh word to use, but I don't know what else to call it when a pure motive is claimed for what is done for convenience, or when principles are bent because it is too much trouble to hold them straight. The adolescent or young adult may not be willing to accept certain kinds of employment or training because of an aversion to what they represent. On the other hand, he or she may simply not want to work at all. I would call it hypocrisy when listlessness is rationalized with a claim of high purpose. Similarly, when parents, by example or by direction, instruct their children to get ahead in life in any way possible, but criticize a particular act that happens to counter their own prejudices, that too is hypocrisy. One might call this innocence, for in each case the "hypocrite" is ignorant of his own behavior. But isn't that what "hypocritical" means—to be insufficiently (hypo) critical of one's own behavior?

Of course we're all in this together, and each of us contributes to the prevailing bad faith. However, the principal reason the adolescent gets off the track, in my opinion, is simply because the adult generation makes the track unattractive.

17

How To Keep From Getting Bored.

Planning your life doesn't mean boring yourself to death. You must build in challenge and excitement.

When about sixteen years of age, I submitted a short story to *Esquire* magazine. The first reader scribbled on the buck slip, "Remotely possible theme." The second reader wrote, "Not for us. Sorry." (I was rather pleased to have gotten past the first reader!) The story was about a labor organizer who was so convincing that he managed to sign up every worker on earth. Having nothing more to do he died, went to Hell, and organized the souls in torment (he did clever things like putting Sisyphus on an eight-hour day). I forget how the story ended.

In retrospect I don't believe that the theme was too far-fetched. Don't some people get senile and die because they have nothing significant to do? There are two ideas worth considering here.

1. In an important sense we are kept alive by feedback, by the observed consequences of our acts. While in general we seem to prefer that the feedback be good news, even bad news is probably preferable to no

93

news at all. It must be extremely boring to be ignored, to perceive that your behavior has essentially no impact on your environment.

2. Parts of the brain have been identified as pleasure centers, and people will do work in order to have those centers stimulated, either directly by implanted electrodes, or indirectly, through bodily stimulation, or by the ingestion of pleasure-producing substances. There are also neurophysiological pain mechanisms, and we are willing to work to *avoid* having them stimulated. Some people seem willing to work to *receive* pain. While it is not yet very well understood how this comes about, on a common sense level it may be proposed that if someone gives us pain, we at least know that: a) we are still alive, and b) there is someone out there who knows that we exist. Probably the modalities of pleasure and pain, through a neurohormonal mechanism, have an important influence on the general tone and well-being of our whole organism. When some speak of "holistic medicine," they probably have in mind the overall effects of pleasure and pain on our general health.

I am not sure to what extent it is true that individuals can literally be "bored to death," but there is doubtless much truth in the metaphor.

Why do people get bored? Is it their own fault if they get into a situation that offers them little or no feedback? Probably not, but it is possible that somewhere along the line they made an error or a series of errors, or possibly their life strategy failed, or perhaps they had no strategy. And now they have no more moves. So, like a ball player no one wants, they play out their option. And die. Of course, since life is imperfect, a miracle may happen. An unforeseen, unplanned opportunity occurs. Something catches on. They get new life. It does not seem like anyone's fault, one way or the other.

A high school student decides that he is getting nowhere with his academic studies and tells his parents that he is switching to the "vo-tech"—the vocational and technical high school. His parents may think this is just fine because he's been wasting his time and maybe now he'll learn something useful, like how to repair air conditioners, get a job, and perhaps even contribute to the family income. On the other hand, they may throw the proverbial fit and scream that he's giving up his chance of ever going to college and becoming something worthwhile.

The student is thus at a choice point. Since this is a hypothetical case, the best choice is moot. We know, however, that the course followed will have an important bearing on later life, and probably on the kind of old age that will come.

Thus we tell our children to keep their options open.

This does not mean that the young man or woman who goes to vocational high school is a sociocultural dead duck; that judgment, if anyone is to make it, depends on decisions made at future choice points. There will be several such choice points, their number is limited. The initial decision to give up the academic course, needless to say, effectively reduces the number of future options.

Since not everyone has the opportunity for wise advice or counseling, it is fortunate that many options reside within ourselves, and are not necessarily part of the formal educational-professional-industrial system, where following the right course at the right school often determines career success or failure. There are still many opportunities for the craftsman or tradesman, and certainly there are innumerable avocational choices. It is absurd that so many of us defer learning to ski, sail, play golf or tennis, paint, or play the piano until acquiring these skills becomes a hardship. In one sense it's never too late; in another, the spirit is willing, but the joints may be arthritic.

It is accordingly possible to define old age as the time

without options. I have seen elderly people as patients who have asked, "What am I to do?" A crippled, bedridden woman in her eighties complained, "It isn't even easy to die."

This is not to suggest that there is nothing to be done with or for the aged. As a physician, I am not devoid of options in dealing with old people. They themselves may have no more life choices.

Obviously, if one is to keep from being bored in old age, the necessary choices must be made *before* old age is reached. One needs a long-range view, together with the realization that old age is a fact of life.

But these are merely the prerequisites. There is a core perception that must be acquired, an image that is both necessary and sufficient, that will set planning in motion.

Wherever you are in your life, at whatever age, you must now stop and return to your final moments as an adolescent, before you made the inevitable move that carried you on to the arduous but comprehensible demands of adult life (in contrast to the often incomprehensible demands of adolescence). What were you thinking and feeling then?

In your adolescence there was a duality of being. You were meeting the formal, realistic demands of going to school, possibly also to religious school, and doubtless taking some kind of "lessons" you probably had little interest in at that time. Simultaneously you dwelled in a land of fantasy. What were you in your dreams? An actor or actress? A singer, dancer, or musician? A super-salesman? President of the United States? A beachcomber? Ski bum? Edgar Guest or Norman Rockwell? The world's greatest lover? What your dream was matters less than that you get in touch with it, whatever it was. In the most favorable case you never lost contact with it. In the second best case you will retrieve it easily. In the worst possible case you will never get back to what you lost, and are doomed to senility. No wonder you are bored!

Theoretically, there should be a condition or state of pure, unadulterated boredom in which apathy is nurtured by a series of uninterrupted, uninteresting stimuli (admitting the implicit contradiction of "stimuli" that don't "stimulate"). Yet it is more likely that the boredom will be contaminated by annoyance, resentment, or anger. (A deliberate effort, like the so-called Chinese water torture, can produce even stronger emotions.) The evident reason for resentment is the realization that things could be better, that something could happen, that there might be news from the outside world, and that the news might even be good! But no, nothing happens, and the boredom grows into anger.

However, it is not only the boring present that annoys; it is also the past. Why does one lose touch with the dreams of adolescence? Were there no dreams at all, or did they seem hopeless? Or has life pounded hope into sand?

18

Never Lose Touch With Your Own Adolescence.

Once upon a time people with great dreams walked the earth. One of them was you.

In Chapter 15 it was proposed that the adult moratorium replaces the adolescent moratorium. We stop worrying about the future of the universe and settle down to the business of keeping our house in order and paying our bills. Instead of dealing with larger-than-life issues, we focus on everyday life-size matters. We become more practical, more pragmatic, less idealistic.

On the face of it, this seems the way things should be. Only devious psychiatric reasoning could find fault with the normal straightforward process of coming to grips with the real world! No argument there. However . . .

To put it bluntly, many of us get so bogged down in detail that we miss the point of existence. We forget what it was that we had set out to accomplish, and we mistake the means for the end. It is not surprising that this funneling of perception takes place, but its predictability makes it no more welcome: it is surely no less debilitating a tragedy than cerebral atherosclerosis in its consequences. Indeed, the two have much in common: one narrows the mind; the other narrows the brain's arteries, which in turn narrows the mind.

The difficulty does not arise simply from the admirable qualities of paying attention to detail and coping with each developing situation. These are traditional virtues, which even the most easy-going among us are quick to recognize. The problem grows insidiously, reaching a critical mass long before we are aware of its existence. We find that we are living defensively, playing a game of catch-up with our time and material resources. We may fall behind with respect to our bodily energy and become "run down" and physically or emotionally drained. We may become ill.

All of this contrasts with the ideal of being "ahead" and "on top of things." "It" is running us when we should be running "it." If we ever had a plan, it isn't working.

Of course there is a strong possibility that no plan ever existed. And without a plan, or without being rescued, there is often no way back to a hopeful, positive existence from a routinized, trivialized existence. *I strongly suspect—though without hard data—that old people who earlier had long-range plans are much less likely to become senile than those who led a day-to-day, reflex existence.*

It must be acknowledged that adolescents are not noted for their ability to develop long-range plans. They may have glorious dreams, aims, or goals, but it is a rare youth who can list the steps leading from point A to point P. Perhaps it is the ability to begin the formulation of plans that marks the transition from adolescence to young adulthood.

But while the formulation of plans is necessary, it is not sufficient. Two essentials must be included in the plans. For this kind of smooth sailing the ship needs two lookouts, one in the bow and one in the stern. It is necessary to see not only where we are going, but also where we have been.

Anyone with experience in planning knows that plans must periodically be updated and sometimes radically altered. This is certainly true in business, but business is different from life. For example, Sam Weems decides that he will be to parsnips what Ocean Spray has been to cranberries and Sunkist to oranges. He is successful in founding Parsnips Cooperative, Inc. Things go well, and at the end of its first planning period PCI decides to buy Boxtop Trucks. Expansion continues vertically and horizontally into oil wells and real estate, PCI splits three for two and two for one, declares extra dividends, discovering meanwhile that there is no longer any sizable demand for parsnips. So PCI gets out of the parsnip business and years later there are only three traders on Wall Street who remember that the "P" in PCI stands for parsnips. But this memorabilium is of no value in helping them to decide whether to buy, sell, or hold.

But life is different from business. Multinational corporations or conglomerates may maintain their identity while losing sight of their origins, but you or I may not. Of course most of us know at least one person who seems to have "invented himself." There are "self-made" men and women who are so mysterious about their roots that they seem to have come from nowhere at all. Some actually confabulate an entire family tree, but that is less serious than to maintain myths or illusions (or even delusions) about one's own childhood and adolescence. What I suggest most strongly is that we are sustained in old age by a sense of continuity throughout our life, what I referred to earlier as "pervital unity." And I don't believe that this can be accomplished by telling ourselves fairytales made up for whatever occasion. In "The Razor's Edge," W. Somerset Maugham created a social snob who decides on flimsy evidence that he is really a "nob." For a while his canard flies but eventually it crashes to earth. By contrast it is delightful to hear W. Buckminster Fuller or W. H. Auden speak of their own childhoods. Of course, it helps to have had a pretty good childhood and adolescence with which to keep in touch, but whatever the truth, it is best that it be known. (There may be exceptions, as in cases of massive physical disability or outrageous crimes.)

I will not deny that truth can be a limiting factor in making plans. To know where one is and where one has come from has more than a little bearing on the kind of aspirations that are within reach. Each of us is free to dream dreams; we are also free to verbalize, generally free to vocalize, and more or less free to attempt to realize our dreams. But we are also free to waste our time in fruitless ventures, to tilt at windmills, or merely twiddle our thumbs. If we know where we are and where we have been, it is not difficult to comprehend that there are some places we probably can't get from here, some that we can if only we can find the way, and some that are probably not worth the trouble.

It may sound unAmerican to suggest that there are goals that cannot be reached if we are willing to pay the price. The struggle for equal opportunity, which is likely to be unending, suggests, however, that reality is unAmerican. And even if there were equal opportunity there would of course remain inequality of ability or aptitude, unless we were all to be replaced by clones, which would rather spoil the game. In any event, the issue is not really whether we can get there from here, but rather if the goal is worth the cost.

I plead guilty to a particular bias about life that I am prepared to spell out. It has long seemed to me that the correct measure of one's life is not the highest point attained, but rather the way the final years are lived, at least to the extent that they are under one's own control. If a heroic figure is cut down by a stroke which renders him speechless and paralyzed—what many of us helplessly refer to as having become "a vegetable"—his final time on earth is clearly not under his control, and ought not be considered in the accounting. But to achieve success by destroying one's associates and family, and becoming dependent in one's final years on what kindnesses may be purchased, represents to me not only a moral and esthetic failure, but a failure of emotion, feeling and spirit.

There is an interesting interplay between the dreams and ideals of the adolescent and the realism or pragmatism of the adult. A fine balance must be maintained or, according to my scoring system, we lose. And we lose because our old age is empty, devoid of prior accomplishment or of meaning, or both. For to maintain the dreams without learning the mechanisms for their realization, or to seek wealth and power without an ethical or esthetic base for their deployment, means either not to get there at all, or not to know where you are when you have arrived.

At this point you may have, as I do, a mental image of an adolescent, perhaps sloppily attired, at least moderately disobedient, scrounging money for a ticket to attend what is called a "concert" by a group of sense-overloading light and sound technicians who do extraordinary, often harmful things, with music and costume. And, we ask, is it this kid's values we have to keep in touch with to keep the rest of our life meaningful? And, crazy as it may seem, the answer is yes.

PART IV

There's Also Good News: You're Lost, But There's A Way Back

By now you've probably figured out that the reason why you're upset about your parents is that you have uncertainties about your own life.

19

Looking At Your Children
Will Help.

*Stop to wonder how your children see you. It will help
you to see yourself.*

If I seem to be singing of Rousseau's "noble savage"
when I speak of the adolescent, it is no mere coincidence,
for we all become contaminated by adulthood. Of course,
at no time were we ever "pure" in an angelic way. The
"nobility" of the adolescent lies in his simple, touching,
annoying, admirable, infuriating certainty about what is
right and wrong, and his willingness to fight for his beliefs.
The objects of his credibility system, the particulars of his
belief and disbelief, are of some consequence in life situations, but for the moment I am concerned not with *what* the
adolescent trusts or distrusts, but rather with the fact of his
capacity for both faith and indignation. The purity of this
system of credibility and advocacy is attested to by the
frequent mismatch between the adolescent's beliefs and
what might appear to be his self-interest. His choice is
between what he considers good and evil, not between
what may seem to be good or bad for him. In its choice of

dilemmas, this quadrilemma would seem to model very neatly the problematics of idealism versus those of pragmatism.

Now let's turn this around. If the adolescent were writing about us, his parents' generation, my guess is that he or she might say something like this:

> They seem to be preoccupied with the kind of impression they make on other people. They want other people to see how successful they are at whatever they do, whether it's at their work or at sports or at taking pictures or playing cards, or whatever. They also want to appear righteous or self-righteous, being on the right side politically, taking the right moral positions, generally being associated with "good" causes. Even the biggest crooks want to look like they're good to their families and contribute money to charity.

In other words, I don't believe that our children see us as individuals concerned with the very difficult struggle of deciding what is good and what is evil, either generally or in particular situations. Instead, they tend to see us as attempting to choose between alternate behaviors, using as our criterion whatever will permit us to look good in the eyes of the beholder. As if this weren't bad enough, they also believe that our efforts to make the smart choice leads us to making the dumb one. In essence, they see us as unequipped to serve our enlightened self-interest.

Doubtless our children can be wrong, as can anyone, yet their eyes are also beholder's eyes and, as beholders go, they're very important indeed. Beholderwise, I would rank them number two. First come our own selves, then our children, then everyone else.

At least that's the way the ranking *should* be. When our children find our choice of behaviors unsatisfactory, it's not because of *what* we've chosen (although our children may not realize this) but because our rankings are reversed:

we are first performing for others, next for our children, and only finally (if at all) for ourselves. If to our own selves we are not true, then to every other individual we must be false, and this troubles our children, even though it may not bother the other individual, who may well be doing as we are doing.

I do not suggest that our children expect to be considered first; that would be more centrality than they're ready to handle. Children find it extremely disturbing when parents tell them, "Everything I do, I'm doing for you." The children think, "Don't put it on us. If it doesn't make sense to you, don't do it."

I must admit that it is difficult to say this even to myself, and perhaps even more difficult to say this to others, because it is so easy to lose friends, but I would be unable to face my idealizing adolescent self if I didn't say it. So I am compelled to share with you my nagging realization that our children are probably right, and that our behavior really doesn't often make good sense for us, and accordingly not for them. We aren't behaving effectively either for us or for them; regardless of whom we think we're doing things for, we're not always doing them well. And there is a reason for this: the unseen audience. I don't mean that the children are right when they say that we're essentially trying to impress our friends and neighbors, because those very friends and neighbors themselves represent a choice. If we seem to be trying to impress friends and neighbors it must not be forgotten that we picked them, we chose whom we would try to impress. We chose to live on Delphinium Drive, Rabbit Run, RFD #3, in Midcity Towers or Haphazard Acres—we chose a particular style of living, and friends and neighbors followed from that choice.

And what determined that choice of lifestyles? (Is the litany becoming familiar?) Yes, good old Mom and Dad. They are the unseen audience. We chose a lifestyle based on what they expected of us (or in 180-degree defiance of what they expected). And how well it works depends on Mother's love.

A few people come from Great Families. A Great Family is one in which the patriarch, Pontius Pirate, manages to stash away enough megabucks so that none of his descendants has to work for money. In the worst possible case, *someone* has to maintain and increase the family hoard. But others are free to become artists, writers, judges, college presidents, senators, bishops—all the good things—without having to venture into the dirty marketplace. But even Great Families don't require many stars per generation to maintain their greatness. A Great Family can sustain 75 to 80 percent dilettantes, drunks, and ne'er-do-wells and still remain Great. In the fine grain of *all* families we see that achievement and a personal feeling of adequacy follow the same principles of meeting parental expectations with or without Mother's love as applied to the Smiths and the Johnsons and the Cohens and the Kellys. We all dance on the same stage before the same unseen audience, and we all do or do not feel good about ourselves. And for the same reasons. F. Scott Fitzgerald was wrong: In the sense of trying to satisfy their parents or not, in the sense of feeling loved or not, the rich are like everyone else. They are different in the sense of believing that if they don't like this world, they can buy a new one. But they can't.

A few people come from Very Talented Families. And some people are Very Beautiful. Yet if they are lacking in the qualities that are admired by the great unseen audience (good old Mom and Dad, again!), they feel like clodhoppers.

And they spend their lives doing—not what will please them—but what they unconsciously feel will please their parents, and what they feel will bring them the love they once had or never had.

And as their children look upon them, what do they see? A source of support? An object of identification?

I recall an episode which occurred many years ago. We were filling out personnel forms and managed to get past name, sex, and date of birth. The next item was labeled "Dependents." My neighbor looked up and said, "Dependents. Dependents? Do I have *dependents?*" He paused. Then he uttered one of the all-time heavy-hitter classic lines: "How can I have dependents? *I'm* dependent!"

Is there a better way to say it?

20

When Everything Becomes Clear.

You exist at the intersect of three generations. When you perceive your own situation, you will know what to do about your parents. It will even help with your children!

At some time during their middle years many people have what is called a mid-life crisis. This anxiety-cum-depression fun-stopper, along with mild heart attacks and breaking one's leg while skiing ("He's lucky it wasn't his neck"), is a member in good standing of a class of near-catastrophes known as Blessings in Disguise. In a mid-life-crisis the futility and hopelessness of existence appears to hang over one's life like an October fog that won't burn off in the afternoon sun. Everything seems wrong mostly because nothing seems right. Self, family, friends, business and one's favorite sport couldn't be less gratifying. The usual scotch, tobacco, food, clothes, bed, bed partner, record, chair, view, painting, pet, tranquilizer, have lost whatever charm they had. Joy has ceased to be. You can't even get a good night's sleep. Some sufferers go on to suicide.

And what, you may well ask, is the Blessing in Disguise?

111

Simply, the opportunity for reflection, reevaluation and renewal of your life.

This is not a Pollyanna viewpoint, nor is it an existential claim that it is better to feel pain than to feel nothing. Perhaps it is to find opportunity in adversity, but more accurately it may be related to Sir William Osler's comment that the way to have a long and healthy life is to have a chronic disorder and to take very good care of it. It is also related to the view held by many psychiatrists that having an emotional breakdown and entering a psychotic state may be desirable in that one is then forced to deal directly with the unconscious, with all of the feelings, fears, and impulses with which one has been out of touch.

If the enthusiasm evoked by this challenging opportunity is miniscule, there is no cause for dismay. After all, if yearnings and avoidances have been kept hidden from one's self for decades, some useful purpose must have been served by their incarceration. We already know the answer to this: the maintenance of the Adult Moratorium.

But do we not wish to continue to preserve know-nothingism? If we no longer remember what we cared about during our adolescence, is it not easier to write it off as irrelevant to the major tasks of life: establishing ourselves in the community and raising our children? Did not W. H. Auden say, "In the end, art is small beer. The really serious things are earning one's living so as not to be a parasite, and loving one's neighbor"? But wasn't Auden a poet and constantly in touch with his youth? So what did he know about the massive repression required by most people to accomplish "the really serious things"? For most of us, who are out of touch, who have lost the touch, art is very large beer indeed. It is heady stuff.

If we can once again see what for so long we have been afraid to look at, we can again reach into the source of our creativity, the reservoir of excitement and involvement that gives life purpose and meaning.

I hear two questions.

1. Is adolescence really the source of excitement and involvement?
2. If so, how do we get in touch with The Source?

The answer to the first question may not seem to be "yes" for everyone. I have talked with a considerable number of people who never had much of an adolescence. Responsibilities were thrust upon them at an early age, and all they can remember readily is having to go to work or having to stay at home with an ailing parent or grandparent. There are others who believe that their adolescence was prevented from blooming by overly restrictive parents.

Adolescence is certainly not the happiest time of life for many. Nevertheless, whatever the reality, there is always ample opportunity for fantasy. And even if you weren't allowed to daydream, you daydreamed. Granted, most of these daydreams were trivial, freeze-dried wishfulfillments (add water: instant ecstasy), but sometimes they took form in a larger scenario depicting a Way Out, a How To Get There from Here. (Depression = You *Can't* Get There from Here.) Such scenarios are not necessarily realistic, and may be more entertaining than practical (unless you can turn them into a movie or TV script), but some are actually the beginning of a life plan.

As I may or may not have made clear, it is these life plans, which often are stillborn, with which this book is concerned. For it is here that we get on or off our life track.

Which brings us to question number two. Can we get back in touch with those aborted plans, can we ever get back on track?

As I see it, the only issue is the choice of return routes.

The first sub-question is whether you travel alone, or with someone's help.

If you attempt it alone, the method is known as introspection. In principle this is the ideal way. In practice the route is fraught with distractions. Most people get lost and end up daydreaming. Perhaps Dante could have visited Inferno without Virgil, but he probably would have become lost. Aeneas fortunately was *fato profugus,* propelled by fate, but Ulysses almost didn't make it back and nearly lost his wife. Nowadays we recommend psychiatry.

Psychoanalysis is the long slow route. Since we're all different, some will prefer to go this way. Most people, having reached middle age, want to get where they're going by the shortest, most direct path. Thus I suggest the following.

Sit with me for a moment, quietly, relaxed, with no sense of urgency. In our time together we have a brief eternity. What was it you wanted? Yes, you wanted to go back in time, back to your earlier time of dreams and incompletely formulated plans, back to where you were before you got caught up in the busyness of adult life. Are you ready now to go back? Very well, you are there. You are now eighteen.

The reason it is so simple is that part of you has always been eighteen and all you have to do is to get in touch with it. And all you have to do to get there is to wish to. It's as easy as ending a sentence with a preposition.

Of course it isn't easy for everyone. Not everyone can perform all the "simple" exercises in the exercise book; our bodies don't all bend the same way, nor do our minds. And of course there are often good reasons for not going back to adolescence. Many people say, "Oh, I could never go through all that again!" Indeed, many adolescences are replete with traumata, and the bad times may outweigh the good. So why go back? I fully realize and accept that some will never go back; even to go back in a dream would be a nightmare. It has never been my job to induce nightmares. So if it's too painful, don't do it. It is always good people who suffer who are willing to suffer more. Don't do it.

But if going back is comfortable for you, if there are pleasant memories with which you can connect, by all means go back. You need to reclaim your identity.

Of course you do have an identity now. Name, rank and serial number. Married or single. Home address and telephone number. Occupation. Next of kin. You're listed in the telephone book, perhaps even in *Who's Who*. You know who you are. The bank will cash your checks.

Okay. If you're satisfied, I'm satisfied. But are you now who you were going to be? When you grew up did you turn out to be what you had hoped or planned to be? If it turned out even better than you expected, I'm truly happy for you. But most people don't stay on track, don't go where they meant to go. Most are not once born and many are never born again. Unless you can be the former, don't be the latter!

I propose that everyone except the once born has two identities. The first of these is the one that is assumed during the Adult Moratorium. This is the alias, stage name, *nom de plume*, pseudoidentity. The true identity is the one that is not realized during the Adolescent Moratorium, which lies dormant awaiting reactivation during one's middle years. If it is called upon, its possessor may be born again, with most desirable consequences for old age. If it is left to wither and die, its possessor will similarly wither and die without ever having found him- or herself.

This is the true tragedy of old age: to have achieved obsolescence without ever having lived.

*　　　*　　　*

In the Preface I mentioned the ancient god Janus, who had two faces, one looking into the future, one into the past. If the rest of us are thought of similarly as having two faces, it might easily be said that the face looking into the future sees our aging parents, which reminds us of where we are going, even as looking back at our children reminds us of where we have been. Indeed we *were* children, and we *will* become old.

It is also possible to say that our two faces are both looking in the wrong direction, or that they're looking in the right direction for the wrong thing. For looking at our parents doesn't tell us where we're going, but where we came from: I refer to parents as the shapers of our developing personality. And looking at our children doesn't tell us what we were like as children; it tells us what we became when we became parents: shapers of our children's personality development.

Thus here we are, deriving from our parental influence, in turn influencing our children. In one sense we are simply a point where two other generations meet. Yet there must also be a third generation: Ourselves, the middle generation, which continues to perceive, act on, and be acted upon by the other two.

It is stunning to note how much of our life is taken up by concerns for the other two generations, our parents and our children, and how little is left for us to be ourselves.

And here is the ultimate paradox: until we know ourselves, we remain absolutely baffled about how we feel about our parents, for all we can recognize is defense and contradiction, love and hate—ambivalence, ambivalence, ambivalence.

21

You Need Help.

A sign of mature good sense is to look for help when you need it. Life is bigger than all of us; we all need help.

In a mid-life crisis, beneath the depression are feelings of loss, separation, and anger. The loss is the loss of one's pseudoidentity; the disguise has been penetrated. The separation is separation from the self that might have been. The anger is at parents who are responsible for or who failed to keep the loss and separation from happening.

Or at least we *feel* that our parents have failed us.

Or we deny that our parents have any responsibility for our plight and take the blame on ourselves. In which case we feel very ashamed and downhearted, and that is what is meant by feeling depressed.

Thus there appear two alternatives: one can be angry at his parents and feel guilty, or he can blame himself and feel depressed.

That neither of these choices is very attractive is immediately evident. However, it is entirely in keeping with a mid-life crisis that the situation should appear hopeless.

Fortunately, the hopelessness is more apparent than real, and there is a way out: to get in touch with one's own youth, to reintegrate with one's true identity.

During the past few years there have been several articles (one I have at hand is from the *Medical Tribune*, a newspaper for physicians) about a neurosurgeon originally from India, superbly trained in America, who gave up his profession to become a sitar player (a sitar is an Indian instrument which resembles a guitar. To be a sitar player in India is a semi-religious calling.) Surprisingly, he reports that some of his American colleagues could identify with his problem, but in India all who knew him thought he was crazy!

For doctors to become artists of one sort or another is not unheard of. Anton Chekhov, W. Somerset Maugham, and William Carlos Williams were trained as physicians, to cite familiar examples. These exceptional men gave up one noble profession for another. Recently, however, I was confronted by a successful salesman who would have preferred to "work with his hands." Could he accept the loss in income? He thought not. It was his choice. I only ask that you get in touch with yourself.

Loss in income is certainly a reality problem, and I am not recommending that anyone commit financial *hara-kiri*. There is such a thing as gradualism, and it is not necessary to close the store and go bird-watching the week before Christmas. There is always a smoother way to make a transition even though there may not be a guaranteed vocational differential.

Nevertheless there can be no doubt that anyone's *machismo* can be strained by being asked to "make it" twice. Success, or even adequacy, is often hard enough to come by the first time. (Incidentally, the feminine for *macho* isn't "facho" or "hembra," but "sin verguenza"—without shame.) But I'm not talking about "making it," or any such self-aggrandizing notion of success. All I'm talking about is getting in touch with yourself, getting back on track.

It is enough to get back in touch, to get back on track. It is not necessary to become a "success." The maturity and sense of reality needed to follow my argument to this point is sufficient to make personal failure unlikely. If the mature adult in his middle years returns to the aspirations of his youth he will not leave his wisdom behind. Each of us has said many times, "If I had only known at eighteen what I know now ..." All we have to do is get back to eighteen and complete the statement. We won't let our family starve.

Indeed the notion of success is not essential to the ego. There is an indigenous need to grasp, to comprehend, and to master. There are needs to acquire and to defend. But to become a "success" and to achieve positions of relative wealth and power reflect attitudes instilled by parental brainwashing, example, or failure.

If success comes easily or comfortably, and if it is compatible with original goals and yearnings (that is, if we are "once born"), there is no headlong plunge into the Adult Moratorium, no assumption of a pseudoidentity, no discontinuity with the true self. In contrast, if one's chosen field (regardless of how the choice was made) provides only an uphill struggle with few rest stops, there is reason to wonder if one may not be on the wrong track.

One way of determining if someone is on the wrong track is to inquire if he or she has considered taking, or has taken, courses or read books on how to unleash the mind's hidden powers, how to become a successful, self-assertive, top banana. Certainly there are reasons other than being off the track, out of touch with one's self, for exploring these areas. However, it may be useful to recall some of the processes involved in the Adult Moratorium. One's aspirations must be repressed, or at least suppressed, and powerful measures of adaptation and compensation must be adopted. It is hard work to build up a pseudoidentity, and all of the ego's mechanisms of defense may be called upon. Sometimes these mechanisms may fail, or may be inadequate, and outside supports are sought. Psychic bandaids may cover only small nicks and scrapes, but their presence marks a veteran of the wars of ego defense (psychic bandaids are recognized by their trademarks: TM, TA, est, etc.).

Perhaps it is becoming evident why a full-scale breakdown (apart from suicidal attempts and other destructive acts) may not be the worst thing that can happen to someone who is middle-aged and out of touch: it provides an opportunity for a major self-reappraisal. Popular movements tell us that it is not necessary to do any intensive self-exploration; indeed, they suggest that it may not be a very good thing to do. Of course popular movements do not attempt to deal with serious disorders of the human spirit. Phenomena beyond mild ennui or discontent are entirely out of their domain.

But there is a more significant difference between psychic bandaids and true exploration of the self. Popular movements are designed to help people maintain their pseudoidentity. They treat the illusions of the Adult Moratorium as though they are indeed the reality that they claim to be. They seek to remove uncertainties and self-doubts, to shore up defenses and to put a smile on our faces; and return us to full duty, business as usual.

The search for the true self teaches us to recognize the arbitrary, often accidental nature of our life course, and to recover our youthful aspirations, when life had purpose and meaning, when we wanted to accomplish something significant for ourselves and perhaps even for humanity before we got bogged down in the Adult Moratorium.

If we can find our way back, alone or with help, there will no longer be a cause for frustration, because we will not be doing what we *had* to do but what we always *wanted* to do.

And if we fail at that, at least we fail at doing something that is meaningful and important to us.

If we achieve a new skill, a new competence, a new sense of mastery, it will be ours, and ours alone. If we fail, we can try again, free of the guilt of having disappointed someone, and without the resentment of having failed to achieve a position to which we never aspired, but toward which we were urged.

Thus with exploration of the self comes freedom. Freedom from what? Freedom from the ambitions engendered within us by our parents, through our parents, because of our parents. Freedom from the need to prove something to our parents, whether through our own success or our own failure.

And with this freedom comes freedom from anger. We no longer have to be angry at our parents, and without this anger we are free to love them as human beings. And since we care for our parents we will regard their situation objectively and be able to make appropriate plans to meet their needs.

Of course, if we were all once-born and able to live our adult lives without sacrificing the dreams and plans of our youth, there would be no need for frustration and anger. But how many humans are so fortunate?

Inevitably there will be some who argue that they are actually better off for having forsaken the dreams of their youth, and they are eternally grateful to their parents for having straightened them out. I won't attempt to respond to that now. But I would like to hear from them when they reach their old age.

22

Your Parents Need Help.

Old age is not second childhood; it is the third adolescence.

Our parents are frightened. They may not say so, but they are frightened. If they are living alone, they fear what the next day, the next hour may bring. Even if they are in the best of health, they see their remaining friends become ill, incapacitated, and die. They suffer the loneliness and even the guilt of being survivors. While both parents are alive they have each other. But when one goes the other is desolate.

They still have us, but they do not have us. As Khalil Gibran said in *The Prophet,* "Your children are not your children." We are persons of our own, we have (or do not have!) our own children, that is, we have them to care for for a time. We are busy, we are occupied, preoccupied. Even if our parents have the "security" of a total care retirement community, they may have many people around them, but no one is close.

Unless they maintain a vital interest in some mental activity their minds will grow slack from boredom, even as

123

their bodies will atrophy without physical exercise. There is little point in telling them to get interested in something, when they tell us that life is without interest. Our suggestion to them to "get interested" is kindly, rational, appropriate-sounding; but it doesn't work. The inner stimulus, the motivation is missing; the necessary ingredient isn't there.

What is the solution? It is for them to get in touch with themselves. I spoke with an old man, almost completely paralyzed with spasms and weakness. Quite intentionally, I asked, "What are you going to do when you grow up?" and from his trail of thoughts and memories he replied, "I never had any plans. I just lived, foolishly, from day to day, and here I am, with the tapes playing backwards."

This, of course, is my thesis, but I had never expected it to be so clearly confirmed, although I had already spent more than one hundred hours "breaking through" this person's dementia. Was he speaking random words that at last seemed to make sense? Had the monkey finally pressed the right keys to compose a sonnet? I think not, and future conversations confirmed my hypothesis. He knew what he was saying and meant to say it.

Of course, for him it may be too late in the sense that there is almost nothing he can *do*, but at least at times he can think straight, achieving a conceptual line from there to here, even though he might never connect the points by action or modify his behavioral thrust into the future. (*Thrust? Future?* The words seem ill-chosen. He would like everything to stop, but the tapes keep running backward.)

It is because the tapes run backward that I persist. Something is being repeated, everything is being repeated. Everything is moving back, but back to where? Is it a purposeless revisiting, or is there a destination? Is there some point to which the tapes are returning? I suspect that there is a point, a choice point, a fork in the road, a switch-point along the track, a time and a place where everything got *off* the track, where things might get back *on* track again, if it isn't too late.

But of course it is too late. We won't have time to finish our work. All that functions now is his mind. His body will soon stop, and then of course there will be no mind. He is apologetic because he can scarcely work with me. I think we may have only a few minutes more. Before he leaves I would like to hear him say that he understands, but he might be saying it solely for me. I would like a sign of his understanding. Or perhaps he does understand, and it may be his final mischief that he will not tell me so. That would have to be all right. It would be a privileged non-communication.

He is past eighty; we should have started sooner.

When should we have started? We should have started "before." But when is before? How early do we start? At the first sign of senility, or earlier? Much earlier. I suggest starting as soon as possible.

Very well. Let us assume that we agree to get help for your parent. Your question is, "How do we get Mother or Father to see a psychiatrist?" I will answer this in absolutely straight, deadpan fashion. Thereupon you may comment, "If only it were that simple," to which I will respond, "It is."

First, the straight, deadpan answer: You tell your parent that he or she has an appointment to see Dr. So-and-so at a particular time on a particular day. This should be done as close to the appointment as possible, preferably just before. Your parent questions, "Why do I have to see Dr. So-and-so?" You respond, "Because your doctor wants you to." Nothing more is necessary. Of course I don't know your mother or father, but I am sure that nothing more is required if you want one or both of them to see a psychiatrist.

Of course if you *don't* want them to go, the situation becomes more complex. But since you *do* want them to go, there won't be any difficulties.

When your parent sees the psychiatrist, it is the latter's job to engage your parent in conversation. In my own practice I have not found it difficult to do this because there are always legitimate topics to discuss.

Naturally I don't expect that your parent will admit to you that he or she is *pleased* to be talking to a psychiatrist. Indeed, it is very much like getting your teenage child to enter treatment. And it is no coincidence that both your parent and your child tend to react similarly. After all, they both have the same problem: What are you going to do when you grow up? There is a slight modification with respect to your parents. In their case the question is, "What didn't you do when you grew up, and let's get in touch with it." The psychiatrist must get in touch with the adolescent in your parent.

There is nothing mysterious about any of this. It is interesting, perhaps, but not mysterious that life seems to be repeating itself, or that issues seem to re-emerge in rhythmic cycles. Life continues to give us another chance. If we are not once born we may be born again. If we do not work out our problems in childhood or in adolescence, we may yet work them out in adulthood or in old age. We seem to work out some of our problems again and again. So there is no need for urgency or panic. If you will pardon the cliché: we aren't going anywhere, so there's no hurry.

What I have to suggest is that *now*, wherever in life we happen to be, is the best time to get in touch, to get back on track. We are always in some phase of a cycle. A "new" experience is inevitably resonating with something from the past. If your parents seem to be slipping away, I wonder if it may not remind you of when you were leaving home or of when your oldest child was leaving home. The weakening bond with your parents creates a sense of imminent separation, and it is not surprising that other significant separations enter your thoughts. You may recall a teenage lover; a heartbreak; despair; black, brooding depression; thoughts of death. It wasn't "the end of the world," but it certainly seemed like it at the time!

*   *   *

As we see our parents growing old, is it not inevitable that we should note signs of our own aging? When I am shaving, do I not sometimes see my father's face in the mirror? A line, an expression, a movement—and then, as he is, it is gone.

How common it is to wonder where we are in life, what we have accomplished, what we may yet accomplish to make it all seem worthwhile! But what we have or have not accomplished is not likely to be considered on its own merits, but rather in terms of what our parents did or did not accomplish, and in terms of what we hope and expect for our children.

I believe that we all need help. We need help for our parents, for our children, and mainly for ourselves. It may be too late for our parents to get help that will be useful for us, but it is certainly not too late for us to get help for ourselves that will in turn help our children.

At times we may wish that our parents had received help much earlier. If we apply this thought to just one generation, it is not too difficult to see ourselves, as parents, getting help in ways that would benefit our own children.

Parents seem inevitably to pass their errors on to their children. It is best for all concerned if the errors are eliminated now. Who needs a dynasty of error!

23

Advertisements For Psychiatry.

If you need professional help, this is why you should go to a psychiatrist.

> *"Things fall apart, the centre cannot hold*
> *Mere anarchy is loos'd upon the world"*

When I recommend that your parents see a psychiatrist I mean a Doctor of Medicine (M.D.) who specializes in psychiatry, who has had residency training in psychiatry and who is likely to be certified by the American Board of Neurology and Psychiatry. A psychiatrist may also have had training in psychoanalysis and may be qualified as a psychoanalyst. However, not all psychoanalysts are psychiatrists, and I specifically recommend that your parents see a psychiatrist. I want them to get the best possible care, and I am recommending the route that offers the highest probability that this will be assured.

Ideally there should be one doctor who is competent to meet the mental, physical and emotional treatment needs of your parents. Such a physician would be a specialist in family practice or internal medicine, with a special interest in geriatrics (the medical care of the aged), and with an additional specialization in geriatric psychiatry. To acquire all this training consecutively, a physician would begin his practice about the age of 35, and he'd be several hundred thousand dollars in debt (even if he didn't actually owe the money, in a bookkeeping sense he'd nevertheless be in the red). Needless to say, this ideal doctor is likely to be a very rare bird. And the time needed for his training would leave very little opportunity to learn about life as his parents have experienced it.

The closest we can ordinarily come to my ideal physician is someone trained in medicine and psychiatry, someone who understands medical practice from the inside, and who also can practice psychotherapy. It is not likely that a skilled psychotherapist will be productively current in internal medicine or surgery, but he will at some time in his training have assisted specialists in these areas. (Some combined internal medicine-psychiatry residencies are now offered.) Moreover, board-certified psychiatrists must pass examinations in neurology (study of disorders of the nervous system).

It is most important that the psychiatrist has delivered babies, participated in surgery, worked in the emergency room, watched patients suffer and die, and had responsibility for the care of patients at all phases of life. It is very easy to overlook this when one imagines the psychiatrist as psychoanalyst or psychotherapist seated behind a patient who is freely associating to his dreams. A psychiatrist is not simply a psychotherapist who is empowered to prescribe medications or electroshock; he is *primarily* a medical doctor, a physician.

Psychiatrists will differ from one another in the extent to which they have remained in touch with general medicine. Some are quite comfortable in treating various physical ailments (so long as they are convinced that the ailments are indeed physical!), while others won't even prescribe aspirin. Some read extensively in many fields of medicine, and attend lectures and seminars in those fields, while others maintain little medical interest beyond psychotherapy or psychoanalysis. Obviously, the psychiatrist I have in mind for your parents is not a stranger to general medicine.

The reason for my bias is simple. I would like your parents' psychiatrist to serve as their primary care physician. He should be the doctor to whom they go with their problems, whether the problems are physical, mental or emotional, or simply problems in living. As primary care physician, he will not be able to deal with all of these problems himself, but he will know how to make a proper referral. He will also be able to confer intelligently with the physician to whom he has made the referral. If several referrals are necessary, the psychiatrist can be the one doctor who is in touch with the others. In this age of fractionated specialization, how nice it is to have someone who knows what's happening to the *whole* patient!

Perhaps you are fortunate enough to have a family doctor who knows your parent well and has known him or her for years. Obviously this doctor is the one to be your parents' primary care physician, and you need not be dissuaded by what I'm saying about a psychiatrist.

The basic need is for *someone* to coordinate your parents' medical treatment. I am nominating a psychiatrist for that role because there is no other specialist to fill it adequately, especially from the mental and emotional, or holistic points of view. If your parents have mental or emotional problems, apart from merely physical ones, the probability is that a psychiatrist will spend more time with them than any other doctor would, and that he will get to know them better as human beings. Clearly, he will be in the best position to evaluate their complaints, to make necessary referrals, to coordinate treatment, and finally to share with you what is going on.

I doubt if it is possible to overestimate the importance of having someone to tell you what is happening to aging parents. When you see significant changes in their behavior, in their apparent understanding, in their ability to express themselves, you can only become perplexed, or even terrified. If only someone could tell you what is going on! Even in cases where little or nothing can be done, it is comforting to know something about the limits of medical understanding and capability. A psychiatrist will provide appropriate orientation. If the one you talk to doesn't express interest in helping you with the problem, have him or someone you respect refer you to another who will be prepared to work with you.

*   *   *

In the final section of this book I present vignettes of some actual cases. Those vignettes are not completely factual, as it is not appropriate that the identity of any individual be recognizable. The problems themselves and the manner in which they are handled by the psychiatrist will be sufficiently real to make it clear that I am not indulging in armchair speculation about the role of the psychiatrist in dealing with problems of old age. Before presenting these vignettes, however, I would like to engage in some armchair philosophizing about human values.

The term "state of the art," or my understanding of it, seems to have changed in recent years. As I used to understand it, it referred to the general level of practice in a particular discipline or specialty, based on current scientific knowledge or available technology in that particular field. Now the term seems to apply to the most recent product, technique, method, or gimmick advertised as superior to its competitors.

In effect, if it used to be fabricated out of metal, it's now made of plastic. If it was formerly made of cotton, wool, or silk, it's now made of polyester. If it used to be repairable, now you throw it away when it's worn or malfunctioning.

Comparably, in the professions, there has appeared a class of partially trained, untrained, or mail order "specialists" tolerated by various state licensing agencies, who claim to be clergymen, therapists, financial advisers, and so on. If you have a problem, there is no dearth of people available to listen to you and make recommendations. You have only to look them up in the Yellow Pages. Doubtless there will be some among these practitioners who are clever or skillful, perhaps even scholarly, in certain areas of human need. And in the absence of evidence to the contrary, there is no reason to question their motives, honesty, ethics, or other qualities of character.

I am willing to consider a hypothetical situation in which you may have the shrewdest diagnostician who is not a psychiatrist, or the most knowledgeable prescriber of drugs, or even the best psychotherapist, not to mention the canniest interpreter of Freud, the most subtle analyst of dreams, or the denizen of the poshest suite of offices. And even if by some computerized magic one were able to mold all of these champions into one non-psychiatric practitioner, I would still recommend that you refer your parent to a psychiatrist.

Unlike Yeats' famous lines, I contend that not all things must fly asunder; there is a "centre" and it does hold. There is a main line of responsible continuity in civilization, and the practice of medicine is the clearest manifestation of this continuity. Thus doctors of medicine are accorded an authoritative status—a status which is reflected in the attitude of the public toward them.

Accordingly, it is correct to say that the psychiatrist has received the highest training that our civilization offers in the many ways in which one human being may professionally care for another. The true state of the art is inherent in the psychiatrist, and when you take your disturbed parent to see a psychiatrist you are carrying out your family role in the most responsible way known to our society. It always feels better to do the right thing.

PART V

How To Find The Answers

The answers are in the back of the book, but they're not really useful unless you've done the work. Anyone may cheat if he wishes.

24

Why There Are Fourteen Ways To Be Old.

Logically there could be more, but there are some empty sets.

In Part I fourteen situations were presented in order to provide a bird's-eye view of the terrain that must be mapped and on which each family's situation may be located. The principle underlying this exercise is that it is possible to make a decision about a parent if you know where you stand with respect to certain specific variables.

Since your parent is going to live in his or her own home, in your home, or in an institution of some sort, and which it will be is a decision you will have to make, you will obviously want to decide in a way that will result in a favorable outcome. The vignettes in Part I showed that under each of the three conditions, parents and children could be reasonably content or quite unhappy, and that no condition could be considered a solution to all problems.

The vignettes also demonstrated that, while money is obviously important, the presence of wealth is no guarantee of a favorable outcome, nor is its absence a sure sign of resulting misery. It is true that it is easier to make a decision when a family is either very wealthy or very poor than when it falls in the middle income range. This is because people in average circumstances often find it difficult to decide just how well off they are and what is feasible for them to undertake. Some average families persist in making decisions as though they were well-to-do and take on too great a financial burden, while other average families see themselves as poor and accordingly subject family members to unnecessary deprivations.

Even though it may be difficult, and not completely free of mistrust and misunderstanding, it should be possible for family members to sit together and calculate how much money is available for the care of their parent. Thus, it is possible to locate one's self along the "money" dimension.

However it is not possible to find a point on a map if one knows only one of the coordinates. Our map is two-dimensional; the first coordinate is money, the second is love. And even as the vignettes showed that money is not all-important, they also showed that the presence or absence of love is similarly an inadequate predictor of outcome.

But there is a special problem in locating one's self along the love dimension, since there are many levels on which we have feelings about our parents and the feelings are not the same on all levels. This is the "Catch 22" that must be surmounted if the right decision is to be reached. For certain conditions require that there be much love, as when your parent is living with you, and certain conditions are tolerable only when there is very little love.

I suggest that here is the nub of the matter. When you know what your family can afford and also how great an emotional bond links you and your parent, the decision follows automatically. On the other hand, if the decision is not forthcoming, some important truth about feelings is being withheld. In that case consultation is suggested.

*   *   *

Once you have decided whether your family is rich or poor or in average circumstances, you have significantly reduced the number of possible outcomes. If your family is wealthy, it follows that your parent may live either in his own home or in yours; there is no need for institutionalization. If, on the other hand, your family is poor, there is no possibility of maintaining your parent in his or her own home, there is no alternative to living with you or in an institution. But if your family is in average circumstances, you still have all three possibilities. Therefore, recognition of how you feel about your parent, and how your parent feels about you, becomes a critical question. If your family is wealthy, and there are mutual good feelings, why should you not all live together? And does not the same situation prevail if you are poor—or, indeed, if you are in average circumstances?

Thus it becomes obvious that you must not mislead yourself. If there is little love, it follows that one should maintain a comfortable distance; the issue is not how your decision will appear to some unspecified audience, but whether or not you will be able to live with it. Of course there are plenty of ill-meaning as well as a few well-meaning people who will find it necessary to tell you or your friends what a shame it is that your old parent wasn't taken into your home. None of these persons has to live with your parent; you do, and only you know what your family can tolerate. *Decisions must be made on the basis of reason, not of guilt.* This cannot be overemphasized; if guilt persists, I do suggest that you see a psychiatrist. It should not be embarrassing to seek help at such a time, and the problem is a non-recurring one.

*   *   *

I have not yet made it clear why there are fourteen situations. I began with three places where your parent might live (your home, their home, or an institution) and three economic circumstances (rich, average, poor). Multiplying the one by the other, nine conditions result. Since any of these conditions can exist with or without love, the total is up to eighteen. But poor parents cannot be maintained in their own home, nor do the wealthy require institutions (with or without love), so the total is reduced by four.

In reality, of course, there are neither fourteen nor eighteen, but an infinity of situations. Each one has its own peculiarities. But having some outline helps to simplify the problem. That's what maps are for.

25

The Parameters Of Decision.

Money, guilt, and fear.

The point I have made repeatedly is that things will only work out if you make a rational decision about your parent. I have also been saying that making a rational decision is not difficult if your father loved your mother and if your mother loved you.

However, even if you're not sure of your mother's love, you will have the problem of what to do with your aging parent, and it is accordingly much more difficult to make a rational decision.

If your mother loved you, you feel good about yourself, you have a successful lifestyle, you know your situation, you know what needs to be done, and you're able to do it.

If you're not sure of your mother's love, you're uncomfortable, insecure, unsure of what you're trying to accomplish, and you engage in a variety of activities whose function is a) to make your mother love you, and/or b) to show your mother what a disaster your life has been without her love. As a result, when it is time to make a decision about *either* of your parents you will go overboard like

Ruth D.'s daughter, or you will tolerate a miserable situation like that of Sophie T.'s children in Chapter Two.

One way of demonstrating how dissatisfied you are with the kind of mother-love you received is by being stingy with your parents. Another way is by spending more on them than you can afford. If you spend more than you can afford you will be miserable. But if you are stingy you will suffer feelings of guilt.

There is only one way of working things out correctly, but there are many ways to do wrong. To make it simple, if you are in average circumstances, you have three choices. Two are wrong, one is right. Which one is right?

I will start by suggesting a situation which seems to be wrong. If you feel unsure of your mother's love, that is, if you doubt that she loves you, if you feel that she has never demonstrated her love for you, if you feel that she was narrow, or selfish, or gave all her affection to someone else, then I suspect that it might not be wise to bring either her or your father to live in your home. (Why not your father? Because if your mother didn't love you, you will hold your father responsible. What if you feel your father loved you? Well, that makes it a little better, but you will still hold it against him that he didn't do a good job with your mother.)

That takes care of one of two possible errors. What about the other? While the other is a little more involved, I think we can work it out by the end of this chapter.

What you want to avoid is a) being stingy, and b) trying to buy your mother's love, because if you are stingy you will feel guilty and if you try to buy her love you will go broke. No rational person will want to be left penniless. Why should you? Answer: to show your mother how miserable she has made your life. Commentary: What would that accomplish? Nothing beyond making yourself miserable.

Being stingy, on the other hand, will make you feel guilty. But what is guilt? Guilt is knowing that you've done the wrong thing. But if you really believed it was the wrong thing you wouldn't have done it, unless you felt you could get away with it. Guilt, then, is fear of being found out. But found out by whom? By others, by people, by the public. But what does that matter? Your friends know what you are like; the "public doesn't care unless you're running for office, in which case you had better not look too stingy." So actually it isn't other people, it's your *mother*. If you're stingy you're afraid that *your mother* will know, and then she'll never love you!

So guilt turns out to be *fear*: fear of being found out, especially by your mother, with the consequence of *losing all possibility* of ever getting her love.

What is clear is that you really *do* care what your mother thinks, so you don't want to be stingy. The only choice is to be objective, to make a rational decision, to calculate the cost of maintaining her in her own home and the cost of a nursing home. If there are other considerations, calculate them too. Objectively. The second wrong decision is, then, to choose on the basis of how your behavior will look to others. The only right decision is the one reached rationally.

Obviously I can't deal with every possible situation, but I can offer one general principle that covers all cases: If you know your circumstances and your options, and if you know how you feel about your parent, you are in a position to come to a rational decision. If your decision is made on the basis of reason rather than emotion, you have a good chance of attaining the best situation available. If you decide on the basis of emotion, you are likely to make a mistake. And this is true even if what you feel is strong love: Don't forget the case of Norma B. and her mother 'way back in Chapter One! And didn't Ruth D.'s daughter,

Peggy, think that she loved her mother? In contrast, consider how well Sally G. and her mother worked things out with no love at all!

26

Living With Your Decision.

This is why you have to do the work instead of skipping directly to the answers.

If you've taken me literally and have actually looked in the back of the book for answers, you will have noted that there aren't any there. The reason why there aren't is that there are no set answers. Any answers that might be there might not be right for you. Actually there are many people willing to provide you with answers. Indeed, everyone associated with the nursing home industry is clamoring for your business, as are the developers of retirement communities. Legions of well-meaning counselors are prepared to tell you that your parents should be kept in their own home as long as possible, while there are doubtless as many who would advise that your own home is the only proper place for them to live. But there can be no set answers, because what will work for your parent depends on how you really feel toward each of them.

"Really," as in the phrase, "how you *really* feel," is a

fascinating word. "Really" can range anywhere from the image you would like to create, to a feeling that became clear to you only after twelve years of analysis. Most of the time, when someone says, "Do you want to know how I *really* feel? Well, I'll tell you," they are either lying to themselves or they are about to lie to you, for they are about to present you with what they would like you to accept as the truth, or what they would like to believe is the truth. People commonly don't know the truth about their own feelings, or else there is no single, simple truth. This is particularly true when we talk about love. Let's look at a few cases in point, going back to earlier chapters in this book.

Sally G. and her mother have achieved a *modus vivendi*. They are rich, her mother is in her own home, and they have accomplished it without love, but through a kind of positive, we'll-make-it-work attitude that keeps things going. If Sally's mother were in any kind of institution, however posh, she would be unhappy, complaining much more about how she was being treated. Sally, not wanting to hear the complaints, would visit less frequently. If Sally had her mother in her own home, Sally would feel imposed upon, and would probably never enter her mother's room!

Norma B., on the other hand, might have tried bringing her mother home with her, or tried to maintain her mother in her own home. This would have required more help in the house, and Norma would have nagged her husband to make more money. But that wouldn't have been Norma's style; individual or couple therapy might have helped.

In Chapter 2, George F. would have made out well anywhere, but Sophie T. would be a storm center under all conditions. Bob and Clara may yet have to take her to a nursing home.

In Chapter 3 Henry P. doesn't need any options; Sara W. doesn't have any.

Moving on to Chapter 4, don't you think that Paul, Lucy, and Walter could use family therapy? I'm still upset about Samuel B.; but this little book can't deal with poverty and crime, and I am not sufficiently naive to think that family therapy will be of much help here.

Ruth D., in Chapter 5, is a classic case which has already been referred to several times. Peggy needs a lot of help. Her husband needs a lot of help. In my office practice I would like to see Peggy once a week, her husband once a week, and the two of them together once a week. But they can't afford the help, which isn't covered by their health insurance. That's another social problem!

Cora Y. and her family, however, don't need any help at all. They are the opposite of a social problem—they are a natural resource!

In Chapter 6, Sonia Z. is a continuing irritant to herself and to others. There is no doubt that she would benefit from psychiatric help. In my practice I would see her regularly because she is depressed; her son Bob occasionally; and her "Keepers" on a p.r.n. basis (*pro re nata*: as needed).

Mary A. causes no one much difficulty; her family, which has gotten rid of her, has problems of its own. Yet no one is seeking help. Nevertheless I feel great curiosity about what went on in their family life. I suspect that Mary A.'s family has a high incidence of alcoholism, and that they have a tendency to ignore their problems (like Mary, they put them away). While all are in need of self-understanding, they do not seek it, and it will not be attained. My profession has no right to impose understanding on them. Another problem.

Finally we have Ben G. and Olga R. If Olga's children had the right or the power to tell her to stay away from Ben, would they have exercised it? Probably not, because they would have hoped that she would have found some happiness with Ben. Ben's having a good time now, but how will he like it when he *really* gets old? I suspect he may die in harness.

*   *   *

Looking back over these cases, it is evident that many of them present no options, but in some cases the choices were not made rationally, but were neurotically determined. About half of the situations could have benefited from psychiatric help, but in some cases the help was needed many years earlier, nearly a lifetime earlier.

I am saying once again that it should not be difficult to make a decision; but *if you don't know what you truly want,* it's easy to make a mistake.

27

Can You Change Your Mind?

Yes, you may change your mind. There may be some penalties.

This chapter and the next may appear to contradict one another; but the apparent contradiction is a matter of timing. In this chapter I say it's very difficult to make a change, and therefore you should be very certain before you make your first move; in the next chapter I say it's very difficult to change, and therefore you must make a move. These statements are not identical in content and meaning; moreover I'm saying one of them now and saving the other one for later. (It's permissible to give contradictory messages, such as, "I'm hungry," and, "I'm not hungry," if you've had dinner in between.)

If we say that all transactions take the form of a contract, it follows that making contracts and breaking contracts are both transactions, but the former is easier than the latter, that is, unless the contract is flexible and allows for its own termination. A rigid contract, on the other hand, resists being broken.

147

For example, let's say that you and your wife or husband are figuring out what to do with your mother when she leaves the hospital after having had her gallbladder removed. She can go to her own home, to your home, or to a nursing home. She was in reasonably good health until she developed gallbladder symptoms, and you had not been giving any thought as to where she would spend the rest of her life. But suddenly you are faced with a decision.

"Well," you say, "it's only temporary; we can bring her home with us for a week or so while she gets her strength back." But suppose two or three weeks pass and she doesn't get her strength back? Or suppose she likes living with you and doesn't want to go back to her place or to a nursing home? You may find that you have made a decision you didn't intend. Try to imagine suggesting to your mother that she move out of your home! It's not an impossible one to survive, but this is not likely to be a confrontation you'll welcome.

Accordingly, you can see why I propose that it's very difficult to make a change, and therefore you should be very careful when you make your first move. You may feel that the example used here is atypical and that you are not usually called upon to make such a hurried decision, but I assure you that this situation is not atypical at all. It is quite common for older people, like cars, dishwashers, and nuclear generators to break down all of a sudden, leaving us with miles to go before we sleep, a sink full of dirty dishes, or a county full of radioactivity—not to mention a house full of mother-in-law. The time to plan is *before* things happen.

If you are married, as most middle-aged people are, I suggest that you look into your marriage contract and see what it says about the care of aging parents. You doubtless don't have a marriage contract, and even if you do, it doesn't say anything about aging parents. When you got married it is most unlikely that you gave the matter an instant's thought. Probably the only thought you had about your beloved's parents was the size of their wedding gift. Little did you suspect how wrong people were when they told you, "You're not marrying her/his parents!" The truth is that you *are* marrying each other's parents (and all ancestors as well, genetically speaking). So it follows that the time to think about aging parents is before you get married. Tell your kids.

It might be argued that if people thought about all the vicissitudes of marriage, including themselves, other people, their children, other people's children, and—oh yes— aging parents, they might not marry at all. And, indeed, many people do not get married. A very common reason for not marrying *is* overinvolvement with one's *own* parents, but it doesn't usually take the form of worrying about how to care for them when they get old. More commonly, the grown-up child is not prepared to give up his emotional dependence on his parents. In any event, even if you don't get married you may still have the problem of taking care of an aging parent. In this case, you can live together or apart, and in the latter instance your parent can live in his own home or in an institution, so the choices are the same as when you're married. The big difference is that you have to decide alone and carry it out alone, which is both good news and bad news.

It all boils down to a very simple truth. In order to be prepared to deal properly with your aging parent, you are going to have to start thinking about it long before it becomes a problem, and long before you would like to start thinking about it. If you don't have a plan, the need to make a decision has a high probability of bursting upon you unexpectedly, and in that case you may be pressured into making a hurried move. If this happens there is greater likelihood of your making the wrong decision, and it's much more difficult to alter a situation once it becomes established than it is to make the best choice the first time.

Yes, there's something very unfair about all this. None of us is qualified for living; we're all lacking in prior experience. But suddenly here we are, we have the job, and we never even made an application!

28

Are There Any Other Questions?

Time may be running out. Sometimes the decision is painful, but it must be made.

The title of this chapter is, in one sense, more ominous than it sounds. In another sense, less. The first sense is reminiscent of the last words of a teacher immediately before passing out the exam booklets, or of an infantry lieutenant just before battle: both imply that there may be endless questions but it is too late to ask them. In both cases, action must be taken now.

To take action, of course, does not necessarily mean that your parent must be physically moved at this instant. Sometimes it is sufficient action to begin formulating a plan. The more time available, the longer the decision-making process, but eventually there is a moment of truth. Which is, in a sense, ominous.

On the other hand, there is no point in looking at the time of decision as though it were Doomsday. It has been my purpose in this book to explore *why* decisions about the care of aging parents often are difficult, not to tell you that they *should be* difficult. Indeed the decision should *not* be difficult; it is only when decision-making is experienced as painful that additional soul-searching is required.

There is another reason why despair is not in order. In many cases older people have been helped by therapy. This is not to suggest that actual physical debilitation can be reversed or even halted. But much of the suffering of the aged is on an emotional basis. Growing old is an emotional stress, and needs to be dealt with in the same sense that stress needs to be dealt with at any age. Here the psychiatrist can be of help, and in the final section of this book, I will share with you some examples of help that was given and received. As was true in Part I, the cases presented are derivatives of actual cases, but are not to be identified with specific individuals. They represent an amalgam of clinical experience.

PART VI

There May Be Further Help For Your Parents

It may be reassuring to know that old people can be helped in a number of ways.

29

It's Not Just Dying In Balance.

Therapy with the aged is for them, not for the mental exercise of the therapist.

Occasionally an older person will ask, "Why do you want to spend time with me? I've lived my life and I'm just waiting to die." Behind this question, which is often phrased as a querulous complaint, is the plea, "Am I worth anything? Can anything be done for me?"

Another way in which the question is asked is, "Is there time to do everything that needs to be done? Am I too old, too set in my ways? Am I too far off course to find my way back?"

There is also a more sophisticated approach that says essentially the same thing. "I know that you psycho-people think that there's something behind everything, and that everything can be analyzed, but do I have to go all the way back to my childhood to find out what's wrong with me now, and furthermore, what good will it do?" The question implies that the exercise is for the psychiatrist, who has a compulsive need to set everything straight so that the patient will die in balance.

155

I will not deny that I enjoy figuring things out, and that I enjoy seeing other people figure things out. I believe there is much satisfaction in getting things straight. It is one of the greatest pleasures of the mind to discover, to reveal the truth, to find out how things fit together.

I must also admit that there are those who seem to derive pleasure (a perverse pleasure, perhaps, but who can speak for others?) from creating chaos, confusion, wretchedness. If one confronts such individuals with the observation that this is so, they become very angry. I believe that this is true of people at any age, that it is not specific for old people. Behind this evident destructiveness is deep rage that does indeed go back to early childhood, and it may be that many of these people are beyond help. However, some can be helped, and it is important that we do not give up on these sufferers. Life has disappointed them over and over again, and when they were small children, they were not at fault. If we abandon them now it will be our fault. Should we allow only death not to disappoint us?

Fortunately, most people are looking for answers. Given time, answers can be found and old age is no bar to problem-solving. It must be noted that the route to solutions may differ from that for younger adults. Thus it would not be appropriate to establish a rule of therapy and expect older patients to follow it.

Since good treatment is expensive, and bad treatment is never cheap, you will wonder if anything is actually happening in your parent's treatment, and if he or she is actually being helped. There are phases in treatment when you are more likely to ask this question and phases when you are less likely to ask. It may be helpful to consider a hypothetical, composite case at this point.

There has been a great shock in your family life. Your mother has had a stroke and is recovering nicely from the physical effects; or she has had an acute episode of confusion and was found wandering in the city streets; or she became severely depressed and made a suicide attempt. In any of these cases she is likely to have been hospitalized for study. The principal focus of the investigation is to determine by a variety of techniques the amount of brain damage your mother has sustained. Concurrently there will be an evaluation of the emotional component, chiefly depression, in her illness. In the case of stroke, organic brain damage is likely to be the major factor, with varying degrees of emotional involvement, while in the case of severe depression the emotional factors may appear to predominate along with certain biochemical changes and little or no brain damage. In the acute confusional episode, there will be a real question as to the relative roles of brain damage and depression.

In any event, continuing psychiatric assistance will be needed during and after hospitalization. At this point you will want to do everything possible for your mother, including speech therapy along with physical therapy; the need for psychotherapy, even if only of a supportive nature, will be evident. Later, when your mother has regained part of her physical function, though little ability to speak, you may wonder if the contribution of psychotherapy is significant, and you may ask the psychiatrist if it is really necessary for her to be seen three times a week. After all, you may comment, she can't have very much to say, even though there may be a lot going on inside her head. In the confusional episode, the need to get things straight will be more apparent, and in overt depression the need for psychotherapy is self-evident, even though chemotherapy or other organic methods may be used initially.

While in any of the circumstances described above the psychiatrist should see your mother almost every day, his judgment should determine how often she needs to be seen later. It is my opinion that he should see her as often as it can possibly be arranged. In all of the instances cited, there are thoughts and feelings that need to be expressed in words. There is a totality of experience that needs to be organized, feelings to be rendered coherent and put into words (verbalized), words to be expressed as spoken language (vocalized). Even if the ability to speak has been impaired by stroke, the feelings can be organized and perhaps put into words soundlessly. It seems to me that this can only help the speech process. Obviously a skilled psychiatrist will try to avoid excessive pressure on a patient; increasing already present frustration will not help.

If the psychiatrist is functioning effectively as your mother's primary care physician, there are other powerful healing influences he brings to bear. He brings continuity, clarity, confidence, and hope. These are not supernatural or mysterious forces conjured up by a witch-doctor. They are perfectly normal sociopsychological effects deriving from the psychiatrist's position as an authority on mental and emotional disorders. With this position come certain responsibilities, and acceptance of the responsibilities confers prestige and influence which attracts others to make emotional investments in him. Thus when he invests substantial amounts of his time in your mother, his seeing her makes her important to herself; the regularity of his sessions reassures her of steadfastness and continuity of care. As they talk together, she achieves an understanding of her condition and, gradually, of herself. As clarity emerges in some areas she is imbued with a confidence that all is not lost, that she retains residual abilities, and that as these abilities are mobilized, her competence will increase and her level of function will approach a satisfactory state. From this emerges hope, and depression begins to lift. There follows a cycle of positive feedback: as her spirits rise her organic condition improves, which in turn elevates her spirits, and so on.

It is unreasonable to expect that our efforts will always be successful, but having tried is in itself a source of support and strength, whatever the outcome.

30

Making Broken Brains Work.

This man made a comeback following a stroke.

Mr. LeBrun was born in Paris, and with his parents and brothers came to the United States as a small child. He grew up comfortably in a suburb of New York City, but had the misfortune to lose his mother before he was ten. The senior LeBrun had a talent for business, and the family became successful importers, the sons participating vigorously in the enterprise. The youngest LeBrun, he who was much later to become my patient, had been named Henri, but was generally known as Harry.

Except for the early death of his mother, Harry LeBrun had it all. Handsome, successful in business and community affairs, he was an outstanding chess player and a boating enthusiast who raced a 16-meter schooner in international competition. He did have marital difficulties, and his first two marriages ended in divorce. At the age of forty, however, he met an attractive, vital, previously married woman of forty-two. After a cruise around the world they embarked on a marriage that lasted thirty years. They had two children, one of whom made them grandparents, a status each had previously achieved independently.

159

When Harry LeBrun was 71, (1) his wife died of a sudden massive heart attack, whereupon (2) he went into a deep depression. The sons of his older brothers took this occasion to (3) force him out of operating control of the family business. A younger woman who had her eye on him tried to cheer him up by becoming the fourth Mrs. Harry LeBrun, but after (4) he had a stroke, she changed her mind and (5) left him.

When his medical condition had stabilized, Mr. LeBrun was referred to me by his family physician. At this point he was very depressed, had muscular weakness on the right side of his body, and a severe impairment of speech.

Mr. LeBrun's voice was reasonably strong but his principal difficulty was in finding the words to express his thoughts. He could recognize objects, as indicated by his facial expression, but he was unable to name them. If I gave him multiple choices, he would make a correct selection; he was not content to accept *any* name for an object or an idea. He seemed to know what I was talking about. When I tested him by saying something nonsensical, he would look at me with disdain, and would try to correct what I had said. Unfortunately, at first he was not able to do better than I had done, so I would have to correct myself to reduce his frustration.

We had plenty to talk about. In addition to the five traumata above, he wanted to talk about his family, chess, boating, sex, books, movies, finance, and politics. We talked about his feelings, his life, his hopes, his terrors. Principally, he wanted to regain speech. He felt his physical strength returning. Would he be able to read, play chess, sail? But, most importantly, would he be able to spend the following winter on the French Riviera?

I explained his condition. First there was his initial depression, then the stroke, then depression secondary to the stroke. We would be able to deal with the depression, but no one could predict how much lost function he would be able to regain. I suggested that we work together intensively for three months, and during that period not worry about the ultimate outcome.

I prescribed antidepressant medication and talked with his family doctor, an internist, and also with the neurologist who had attended Mr. LeBrun during his hospitalization immediately following the stroke. With Mr. LeBrun's permission I also discussed his situation with his son and his housekeeper. Everyone was cooperative. Would the natural healing process also cooperate? Fortunately his general health was good. I believed that we had a chance.

There were, however, two strong negative factors opposing satisfactory recovery. The first of these was the uncertain nature of damage to the central nervous system. Very little spontaneous repair is expected of damaged brain tissue, and our knowledge about the ability of the older brain to establish new circuits is limited. Especially in older people, doctors tend to be pessimistic about the development of new routes for neural impulses. Scientifically, I share these concerns, but in my office, with live people, I tend to be more hopeful. A guarded optimism is helpful to me and to them.

The second negative factor was the depression. In a straightforward way, Mr. LeBrun made me understand that he did not care to go on living unless his condition markedly improved. Initially he was agreeing to stay alive for three months. We shook hands on it.

Naturally I could not rely on the antidepressant medication to cure the primary depression. If that particular medication didn't work I could increase the dose or prescribe a different drug. But that would be time-consuming. We could not afford to wait and see. Accordingly, I decided to intrude on the privacy of Mr. LeBrun's mental and emotional mechanisms in a forthright, therapeutically aggressive way, somewhat analogous to surgical intervention in a case of suspected appendicitis, rather than wait passively for developments.

Active psychotherapeutic intervention requires a hypothesis. It is not absolutely essential that the hypothesis be correct, but it must at least be capable of modification. Often therapy seems to go better if the hypothesis is slightly wrong, but that depends on how skillful the therapist happens to be.* In any event, I decided that the key word was "wife," so I said, "Let's talk about your wife."

Harry LeBrun's face brightened. He said, "Wh. . . ."

I said, "One witch?" He shook his head disdainfully. I tried again, "Which one?" He nodded. I said, "The real one."

"He died." He shook his head, corrected it: "She died."

"He died, she died, She died, he died. Your mother died. Your wife died. You died." I pushed all his buttons.

"She was the only . . ." Harry was talking spontaneously, but he got stuck. He started again. "The others . . ." He shook his head.

There were two kinds of women in Harry's life. His mother and his wife of thirty years were substantial, matronly women. His first two wives, his would-be fourth, and most of his various girlfriends had been flashy, seemingly sexy, generally clever, but not quite real. The "real ones" were his wife of thirty years, wife #3, and his mother.

I nodded, and spoke directly to Harry's shorted brain circuit. "She died, you died. Your mother died, your wife died, you died."

Harry looked at me steadily and nodded. I had agreement on the level of greatest condensation. Could I ex-

---

*I am reminded of an admirer of the pianist Artur Rubinstein, who, when told of the artist's frequent mistakes, responded, "But *what* mistakes!"

pand—or rather, how far could I expand—and not lose his understanding?

Harry beat me to the punch. "My wife died—like my mother died." He had added the one word "like," expanding the collapsed engrams into an analogy. We had moved a step forward. I had not made him move beyond where he was ready to go, but I had been present at the instant of movement and had provided a stimulus.

Sometimes I urged movement to a place he was not ready to go, but at the end of three months Harry signed on for another three.

"What the hell," he said.

"Right," I said. "What the hell. You can *always* kill yourself. There's no hurry; let's wait until we get stuck." Harry grinned.

We played chess. I am sufficiently bad at chess that there was no need for me to say dumb things like "one witch." I opened. He opened. I made another move, and was already in trouble. The only way I could survive was by being aggressive with my queen: Harry was a sucker for overbearing women. When she was demure he ate her up. If I tried to protect her he ripped through my defenses. If she moved out alone, he would provide a pawn for her to walk on. When he permitted my queen and a rook to enter his rear rank, he looked hurt and confused. There were three times when he could have taken her. I commented on his delicacy and did not win another game.

Finally, as the right side of his body regained its strength, we played tennis. He lacked power, but had skill and experience. He regained his confidence.

He listened to recordings of books and began to read along with the recordings. Gradually he began to read alone.

We made another deal. "Harry," I said, "if you're not ready to go to the Riviera alone next winter, I'll go with you." What could I lose?

Harry went to the Riviera. I stayed in my office.

31

A Case Of Depression.

It's often hard to tell how much is brain damage and how much is mental depression.

I must confess to feeling uneasy about being asked to give a "second opinion." Doctors, like other people, may understand cases differently, and their therapeutic approaches may reasonably differ, but there is always an implication that the first doctor's opinion is perhaps not quite right when a second opinion is sought. Objectively, it makes good sense in certain cases for a patient or his family to seek the opinion of more than one physician; my subjective reaction is based on a belief that doctors should do everything possible to help people, and that the second doctor is called upon somehow to extend himself to do more than the first. If you're Number Two you have to try harder. Perhaps because in such situations the doctor being consulted does try harder, he may occasionally become the patient's new therapist. When this happens to me I may feel momentarily guilty that I "stole" the patient, but more often it is the patient or the patient's family who want to make the change; occasionally doctor Number One is de-

165

lighted to be able to drop a frustrating case. In any event, the knife cuts two ways, and I've certainly had some patients second-opinioned away from me.

Thus I was not overjoyed when a middle-aged man I had helped through a divorce asked if I would see his depressed mother. She was in treatment with a doctor I did not know personally, who proposed to treat Mrs. Gray with electroconvulsive therapy. He planned to give unilateral electroshocks (i.e., to one side of the head), with sedative and muscular relaxant premedication, and with inhalant oxygen before and after treatment, three times a week for two or three weeks. The treatments were to be given in a highly regarded hospital, so there was no basis for concern on that score; I had every reason to believe that the ECTs would be competently administered. A woman of seventy years, the patient's physical condition was apparently satisfactory to permit her the treatments.

There is nothing wrong with prescribing ECT for very depressed older people. If the patient's general condition permits, it is an efficient, cost-effective treatment. However I don't personally prescribe ECT, although I would if I felt it to be life-saving. I explained this to Mrs. Gray's son, and agreed to see his mother one time and offer an opinion.

After seeing her I did not recommend shock treatments. Mrs. Gray was very sick, but I found her to be as much paranoid as depressed, and it seemed to me that there was evidence of organic brain damage. I suggested further study by a neurologist. This recommendation was followed, and a diagnosis of Alzheimer's disease (senile brain deterioration) was reached. The neurologist and I agreed on antipsychotic medication for the paranoia and depression, and I told doctor Number One what we were doing. He accepted our findings graciously.

I do not know that any harm would have resulted had ECT been administered, but the presence of brain damage dissuaded me, since the paranoia and depression did not seem life-threatening.

The medication we employed was reasonably effective, and in a few weeks I was seeing Mrs. Gray in my office as an outpatient. Some doctors find it most congenial to treat patients in a hospital, in their office, or on the couch. I find it most congenial to sit face to face with the patient (individual, couple, or family), preferably in my office, or occasionally in the patient's home when scheduling permits. So I felt that we had moved a significant step forward when Mrs. Gray was able to keep an office appointment.

She was scarcely in the door and only halfway into her chair when I boomed cheerfully, "Well, how are things at city hall?"

She stiffened for an instant before lowering herself onto the cushion, regarding me dourly. Nodding her head as if in pity, she said, "You think it's all very funny, but the mayor—and his wife—are going to make it very bad for me."

"I'm sure they could, if they were so inclined—and had nothing more urgent to do."

"They will. They're very vindictive people."

"But you could charm them," I suggested.

Mrs. Gray's face sweetened, and she flashed me a gentle smile. "But they don't deserve it."

I didn't refrain from responding, "That's what I was telling you in the hospital!" She had regaled me with a confused array of plots and counterplots, the outcome of which seemed to be that the mayor—or especially the mayor's wife—would have her sold into prostitution.

"I don't know *what* you were telling me in the hospital. You had me so full of drugs. Or what I told you," she added, more to the point, since she had treated my comments with disdain, considering me an ignorant supporter of the status quo. Fortunately, she had thought me uninformed rather than malevolent, or we would have been unable to work together on an outpatient basis.

Mrs. Gray's memory was severely impaired, but she was a very proud woman who would acknowledge no deficit. When she could not recall something she would sit in glowering silence, as if putting the blame on the missing bit of information for having absented itself. But she didn't forget the mayor and the mayor's wife.

Our weekly sessions continued for some months and I was able to reduce and finally to discontinue her medication. As Mrs. Gray's thinking improved, the role of the city's chief executive and his spouse diminished in importance. After forgetting why she was furious at them (feebly attempting to confabulate implausible reasons), she eventually forgot her anger.

One day she came in with a coy smile. After leading me up and back several blind alleys, Mrs. Gray confided, "I've met a man."

When I expressed no interest, she told me the whole story in great detail. Then she wanted me to talk with "the man," apparently to get my approval for the relationship. He evidently wanted to meet with me, and I agreed to see him. Mrs. Gray told me that he was eighty-two and in good condition. She implied some urgency. I could understand why she might be in a hurry, but my conservative training signaled caution.

Nevertheless Mrs. Gray's intended and I did meet, and as I had told Mrs. Gray I would, I tried to explain her medical condition to him. He claimed to understand, and advised me of his intention to move in with her. To do so represented no opportunism for him, as he had several other options, and was not simply looking for a place to live.

Mr. Black moved in with Mrs. Gray, and the first report contained only good news. Mr. Black said he was "as happy as a young boy," and when Mrs. Gray next saw me she was smiling contentedly. "He thinks I had an orgasm," she offered.

"Well, did you?"

"I might have. I've never been quite sure."

It occurred to me that if she were able to pay more attention to her own bodily sensations two results might derive: first, she would know whether she was having an orgasm or not; second, she would be more likely to have an orgasm. I would have preferred to discuss with her the problem of hyperalertness, of being overly concerned with what the other person is up to rather than with knowing her own feelings, but the time was not right.

For the next two weeks the news continued to be good, then there was good news and bad news. Finally Mrs. Gray came in and slumped dejectedly into her chair. "We had a fight. I told him to get out and he left."

"What happened?"

"Nothing happened. I made it all up. I picked a fight with him and he left. Is that what you want to hear?" she shouted, her voice bitter with sarcasm.

"No. I'm sorry."

Mrs. Gray was silent for a time. Then she looked squarely at me and said, "You blew it."

"I blew it?"

Mrs. Gray's face became that of the littlest girl she could contrive. "I talk to myself."

"When you blame me you're not blaming me? You're talking to yourself and blaming you?"

Still with the little girl face she nodded.

"And it isn't him or me or the mayor? It's you?"

She nodded again.

She had just discovered paranoia.

"Is it too late?" she asked, once again her own age.

"It's too late for the past," I replied gratuitously, "but—" I glanced involuntarily at my watch—"just about the right time for the future."

"How about the present?" She leaned forward aggressively.

"What?"

"Now. You and me."

"Are you making a pass at me?"

"I'm only teasing you," she said, "I don't want to be back on medication."

I really didn't think that Mrs. Gray was kidding, but she seemed to be handling herself adequately.

"You're sending me out to the meat market," she half-joked.

"You'll do O.K." I said. "I'm more worried about the men."

"Do you mean that I'm dangerous?"

I shook my head. "You *act* dangerous."

"Then we'll have to work on it," she said, grumbling. "To think that I have to start working on this when I'm seventy years old!"

32

Neurosis Revisited.

Sometimes old people are neurotic just like young people.

Several patients with marital problems and small children have independently told me the story of the ninetyish couple who waited to get a divorce until their children had died. I'm sure that grim humor has a place (not necessarily in this chapter!), but there is certainly nothing funny about elderly parents outliving their middle-aged children.

A possibly more distressing situation exists when older people in reasonably good health have middle-aged children who are chronically or incurably ill. It is frequently difficult to deal adequately with the parent's unjustified guilt feelings at such a time because of the often over-powering reality of their son's or daughter's suffering. There is no doubt that every parent can find some fault with his or her parenting performance, but can he or she draw any logically supportable line connecting parenting with the child's illness? There must always be a fallacy in the reasoning process, but the inescapable presence of

171

debilitating disease, which the parent is powerless to alter, makes the psychiatrist's delineation of the error merely plausible to the parent, probably not convincing, and all too often resulting in no change of attitude or elevation of mood. "You're probably right," says the parent, "but I don't feel any better about it." I don't believe that such a statement is necessarily true. The parent may feel better when the lack of causality is clarified, but he or she doesn't *want* to feel better because his or her child is suffering. A 68-year-old widow just doesn't feel right about spending the winter in her condominium in St. Thomas while her 50-year-old daughter is dying of leukemia in Milwaukee. That the daughter wants her mother to go seems only to make matters worse, since it "proves" she hasn't been a good mother.

Many of the same issues emerge, possibly more clearly, when the daughter is seemingly trapped in a repetitious pattern of self-destructive behavior. If the daughter is emotionally ill, the mother feels even more responsible then if her daughter is physically ill, since the causal links seem more obvious.

One mother, a stylish seventy-five, became severely depressed two years after the death of her husband. When I saw her she was chiefly concerned about the plight of her daughter, forty-five, depressed, frantic, deeply in debt, in the midst of a divorce from her third husband (two children by him for a total of five). My patient referred to her soon-to-be-ex-son-in-law as a "skunk," and to her daughter as a harassed, lovely woman. I had no way of validating these judgments, but my patient was a distraught, lovely woman, and it seemed plausible for her daughter to be lovely and harassed.

The term "extravagant" is also a value judgment, but my patient took refuge in the First and Fifth Amendments to the Constitution of the United States when it came to spending money: she considered doing so her *right*, and she refused to talk about it. It became evident that these attitudes were embedded in her daughter's superego formation: mother and daughter considered them to be facts of life; their husbands may have disagreed.

But why had *my* patient been extravagant? Had she also learned it with her mother's milk? No she had not. Her mother, indeed, had been quite frugal. She had even been frugal with her mother's milk, with her mother's love, and with the production of connubial bliss. Thus my patient's father had showered his daughter with gifts, and she became accustomed to getting *things* instead of affection. Her daughter had been brought up with similar expectations.

Why was my patient depressed? I learned that she too was having financial difficulties, and that problems prevented the settling of her husband's estate. It became obvious to both of us that her depression would lift once the executor's duties had been fulfilled, but neither of us cared to wait so long. My handling of her case was not much speedier than the estate attorney's, but my focus was on the development of her emotional responses, their repression, and on the substitution of material goods for emotional goods. Within a few years she was a wealthier, and also a somewhat warmer person.

Having considered a mother-daughter situation in which the mother attributed her own distress to that of her daughter, I would next like to make some observations about the lady whose daughter was dying in Milwaukee. As Mrs. White phrased her complaint, "She doesn't even want to see me, she wants me to go away."

I suggested that the daughter might simply be trying to spare her the cold Northern winter, that a) her daughter needs her but is being stoical, or b) her daughter doesn't need her and is even willing to pick a fight to get her mother to go South.

Naturally Mrs. White wouldn't buy this. Her position was that her place was with her daughter, and that it was ridiculous for anyone to expect her to have a good time while her daughter was in pain.

While I was not privileged to know the daughter's mental state, it was not difficult for me to imagine reasons why she did not need or did not want her mother around. However, I could see no good reason for Mrs. White to cancel her plans to go to St. Thomas. Her insisting on staying near her daughter simply did not make sense to me. (I am very much aware that I have never been, or ever will be, a mother. But I do not believe that being a mother requires or permits one to stop making sense. I expect that some of us may not agree on this point.)

As Mrs. White talked about her daughter, it appeared that they were accustomed to being quite close. The daughter had been an extremely active woman, and even in her illness continued to meet many of her commitments. However, mother and daughter used to spend much time together, although never enough to satisfy Mrs. White. I wondered if I were hearing evidence that the daughter had been trying to pull away for some years.

When I began to inquire about Mrs. White's relationship with her own mother I got a response for which I was not prepared. After the death of her father, Mrs. White took responsibility for the household. As her mother became increasingly debilitated, Mrs. White devoted herself to her care; this continued well into her own marriage. Indeed it required great effort on Mrs. White's part to pay sufficient attention to her husband and to her mother so that neither of them would feel deprived. Was her own daughter neglected as a small child? Mrs. White thought not. She had adequate time and adequate help in the household.

When I asked Mrs. White how she felt about all the devotion she had shown her mother, she expressed surprise that I would even ask the question. "Why, that's the way things are," she said. "Daughters take care of their mothers."

"And mothers take care of their daughters."

"Yes, when I was small my mother cared for me."

"And when she was older and sick you cared for her. Only here you are again taking care of someone."

"But she won't let me take care of her!" Mrs. White had tears in her eyes.

"And when you get older you'll have no one to take care of you."

"But," said Mrs. White defensively, "I don't need anyone to take care of me. I'm—knock wood—in very good health!"

"Precisely," I agreed. "You don't need anyone to take care of you."

"But my daughter needs someone."

"She has her husband and children and as much nursing care as is required. She doesn't actually need you in that sense."

Mrs. White was thinking. "Of course if she ever did need me I could get up here in a day or so. Maybe less."

As I saw it, Mrs. White was doing her daughter a favor by going South for the winter. The daughter would never be able to take care of the mother, and certainly didn't need to be burdened by guilt fostered by maternal overconcern.

In both of these cases the mothers presented themselves as distressed about the welfare of a daughter. While this distress was real, it was also understandable. On further analysis the concern is seen as self-directed. This too, is as it should be. It turned out that both daughters were relieved to have their mothers let them handle their own affairs. This may be a relief to all of us: the distressed middle-aged children might be our brothers or sisters; indeed, they might be you or me.

33

The Best Time Of My Life.

Death can be beautiful.

Lucy was the daughter of a public figure, and like her dad she had been a rebel and had a way with words. But when she was about thirty she had a life-threatening disease and was given an antibiotic that damaged her auditory nerve, leaving her with very little hearing. She learned to lip-read. The next thirty years were relatively boring, but she raised a family and maintained a charming home. However, she felt that she had never quite gotten organized, and that she had failed to achieve the potential of her youth. She looked to her husband and to others, including psychiatrists, but no one had been able to help her put her life together. Because she was so charming there were many who tried to help her, and many others who would have been glad to try, but it was as if no one could uncover what she sought. It seemed to many that Lucy had a mystical quality, that she was reaching for the unattainable.

When I saw Lucy she was miserably depressed. She had had part of a lung removed; although the cancer had not spread, her recovery was slow and there were complications which left her physically debilitated. Furthermore, her husband was seriously ill with coronary artery disease and was currently hospitalized. Although all of their children were married, the marriages were not without problems, and Lucy had concern for her grandchildren as well.

But she had not given up. In her charming way she told me about the men she had known and about her previous psychiatrists. For good measure she threw in that she now had an appointment with another psychiatrist who was going to hypnotize her so that she would be able to give up smoking.

What impressed me about Lucy was her sense of priorities. In the midst of her troubles she never forgot that "the game" came first: the interpersonal game, the man-woman encounter, the politics of being a patient. I was pleased that she was so engaged, and she felt my pleasure and it pleased her. Without my having made an issue of it she stopped seeing the hypnotist and interpreted her latenesses as part of a struggle with me.

The depression was no problem. Lucy felt good seeing me and we laughted a lot. I told her she was depressed because her longest-run lover had married another woman ten years ago and she had felt jilted. This got her mind off her present troubles and because of the distance in time, made protracted grieving impractical. The big issue that we had to deal with were authority and organization. Before her deafness she had thwarted authority, and afterwards authority became nonexistent for her. In minor ways she had been able to organize her life around work, to some extent around her husband, and to a greater extent around her children, but especially since her deafness, she suffered from the absence of a unifying principle.

Inside of a few weeks I felt a marvelous rapport with Lucy. Her voice was somewhat hoarse and she had some difficulty speaking. Lip-reading was not always satisfactory, and I often found it awkward to speak in the range where she had residual hearing. We both very much wanted to communicate and we had decided that we would be able to do so, thus we developed an intuitive understanding of each other. Since Lucy had been psychoanalyzed, I adopted the gambit of assuming that she knew various things about herself, and I would appear surprised when she let me know that it was all news to her.

One day I said, "I'm sure you realize why you've accepted no authority since your deafness." She was sure she did not. "Your father's voice," I said. "You stopped hallucinating your father's voice in your mind's ear." That sounded so crazy to her that she laughed and clapped her hands like a child. Her father had died before her deafness.

"But," she said shrewdly, "just because I became deaf was no reason not to hear my father's voice in my imagination!"

"Exactly right," I responded. "That's where you made your big mistake. You certainly could have kept hearing it, but you didn't. Because you were angry," I added, anticipating her next question.

"Because he had died," she continued thoughtfully.

"And because authority prescribed a drug that later made you deaf, thus discrediting itself."

We pursued the theme that her childhood had been organized around her father's voice, which, when stilled, left her with no focus.

"I've always loved men who would talk with me. I loved to talk and talk with men."

And so we talked, but talking was not always easy. When we had to pause we would smile at each other.

Lucy had had an earache for about a year. Her dentist made her a bite plate so that she wouldn't grind her teeth. He suggested that the earache might be from pressure on the temporomandibular joint. Her otolaryngologist prescribed decongestants. Sometimes she took seasickness pills when she felt dizzy. Nothing helped very much. Lucy feared the return of a laryngeal cancer that had been removed sixteen years earlier.

When laryngoscopy was performed it was found that there was swelling around her larynx. Steroids were administered but they didn't help much. A biopsy was performed. The cancer of her larynx had not returned, but there was cancerous tissue around the larynx. Lucy pressed for answers and was told that she had ten months to live.

She wanted to reduce her sessions with me. Of course I wanted to know why, and she said that she was feeling too dependent on me.

"So what?" I asked.

"I'm getting so weak I won't be able to come here much longer. I'm spending most of my time in bed."

I didn't see a problem. When she could no longer come, I would see her at home. She smiled and snuggled into her chair.

Now we could get down to business.

Lucy told me of a fantasy she had. "When I can't get to sleep at night I think of a beautiful calm lake with dark unruffled waters. There is a forest around the lake, and in the distance there are snow-covered mountains. In the forest are deer and foxes and squirrels and opossums and many kinds of birds. I am in a canoe, but I don't find it necessary to paddle. There is a force driving the canoe."

I waited.

"There is some tribe somewhere that puts its dead into a canoe and lets them drift."

I nodded.

"A year ago after part of my lung was removed I thought I was going to die. I was surprised that I didn't. Now that I know I'm going to die everything is peaceful. I'm completely self-indulgent. I do exactly what I want to do. I read,

I write, I don't cook meals, I talk with the people I want to and not with anyone else. I say what I think and I don't have to fight my feelings. This is the best time of my life."

I never told this to Lucy, but I felt that authority had returned to her life. Her life was now completely organized. Death—and her expectation and acceptance of it— was the organizing principle.

Lucy did not want any heroic efforts made in her behalf. She was given as much medication as she wanted to make her comfortable. Finally breathing became difficult, and it was recommended that she be hospitalized so that a tracheostomy might be performed.

Lucy discussed this with me rationally and in good spirits. She didn't want to have it done, but decided that she might as well try it and see how it worked. We laughed about how she could plug it up with a cork if she didn't like it.

I visited Lucy in the hospital after her tracheostomy. She was unhappy with it and had decided not to go on living. I chatted with her and with one of her children who was visiting.

That was the last time we talked.

Epilogue.

Putting It All Together.

I would have preferred to write this after having heard from you, because I would then have been able to respond to your questions or comments. As it is I can only guess at what you may be thinking, feeling, or saying. I'll do some guessing.

My first impression is that some will say that I haven't told them what to do, but rather have taken them on a long, circuitous trail leading back to where we started. That is correct, and seems to me completely proper. You *should* make your own decisions. My contribution is to provide new information, or better, a new point of view from which to conduct your deliberations. Even if you are psychologically sophisticated, some of the material in this book will be new to you, and you will have noted that nearly all is presented from a new perspective.

My second thought is that you may not agree with everything I say. That is why it's unfortunate that we can't talk with each other, because then I would attempt to clarify my position (or you might convince me of yours!).

Finally, you may be of the opinion that it isn't necessary to understand your own feelings in order to make decisions about your parents. This is very much a matter of style. I would want you to know your feelings if you were buying a house or making an investment in stocks or in commodities. But there *is* a proviso: If you're on a hot streak, *don't* stop to think, just keep going, because your intuition is right. The time I'd want you to do some analytic work would be after your hot streak had ended and things were no longer breaking right. Then perhaps we could figure out what you were doing right before and what you're doing wrong now.

But in any event the secret, as I see it, is to be in touch with your own feelings. I like the phrase "to know where you're coming from"; it isn't elegant, but it "says it all."